"Nicole O'Dell is back with a fresh series to help tweens and teens make godly choices. As a mom who works with tweens, I know just how girl/boy-crazy this generation is. I'm thrilled to have another tool in my arsenal! I can't wait to read this book with my daughter and use it to help us have key discussions about a critical issue to all teens: dating."

—Cara C. Putman,
multi-published author of *Stars in the Night*

"Talented author Nicole O'Dell has created a book that is a must-have for every family. Her fresh insight and voice of experience will speak to tweens/teens and parents alike."

—Jenny B. Jones, award-winning author of the
A Charmed Life series and the Katie Parker Production series

HOT BUTTONS

DATING EDITION

Nicole O'Dell

Kregel
Publications

Published by Kregel Publications, a division of Kregel, Inc., P.O. Box 2607, Grand Rapids, MI 49501.

The authors and publisher are not engaged in rendering medical or psychological services, and this book is not intended as a guide to diagnose or treat medical or psychological problems. If medical, psychological, or other expert assistance is required by the reader, please seek the services of your own physician or certified counselor.

All Scripture quotations, unless otherwise indicated, are taken from the Holy Bible, New International Version®, NIV®. Copyright © 1973, 1978, 1984, 2011 by Biblica, Inc.™ Used by permission of Zondervan. All rights reserved worldwide. www.zondervan.com

Scripture quotations marked AMP are taken from the Amplified Bible, Copyright © 1954, 1958, 1962, 1964, 1965, 1987 by The Lockman Foundation. Used by permission. www.Lockman.org

Scripture quotations marked NKJV are from the New King James Version®. Copyright © 1982 by Thomas Nelson, Inc. Used by permission. All rights reserved.

Scripture quotations marked MSG are from *The Message*. Copyright © by Eugene H. Peterson 1993, 1994, 1995, 1996, 2000, 2001, 2002. Used by permission of NavPress Publishing Group.

Library of Congress Cataloging-in-Publication Data
O'Dell, Nicole.
Hot buttons / Nicole O'Dell. — Dating ed.
     p.   cm. — (Hot buttons series)
Includes bibliographical references (p.   ).
1. Parenting—Religious aspects—Christianity.   2. Child rearing—Religious aspects—Christianity.   3. Dating (Social customs)—Religious aspects—Christianity.   4. Christian teenagers—Conduct of life.   I. Title.
BV4529.O3425   2012   248.8′45—dc23   2012008238

ISBN 978-0-8254-4240-7

Printed in the United States of America
12 13 14 15 16 / 5 4 3 2 1

The Hot Buttons series, as a whole, is dedicated to my mom, who had to deal with more hot buttons when I was a teen than she'd care to remember. Also to my six children, who have so graciously provided the research I needed to write these books . . . whether I wanted them to or not. And to my husband, Wil, who somehow managed to make my teen years look like a walk in the park.

Hot Buttons Dating Edition *is dedicated to my oldest daughter. Natalie, you're proof to me that parents can earn the respect of their kids and that teens do take their parents' advice. I can't thank you enough for respecting the boundaries I've set, seeking to understand why they're important, and sharing our decisions openly with others. You are an amazing young lady, and I pray daily that your husband is out there somewhere, as focused on his future with you as you are on yours with him.*

➤➤➤ *You don't really understand human nature unless you know why a child on a merry-go-round will wave at his parents every time around—and why his parents will always wave back.*

—William D. Tammeus

Contents

Part Four: Parent-Teen Study Guide

Preface

My parenting is very different from my painting. When I paint a room, I open the can, grab a roller and have at it. Much to my husband's chagrin, there's nary a roll of tape to be found nearby. My bare furniture stands trembling as teeny specks of Toasted Almond Satin float to the ground. Why don't I take a moment or two to protect my belongings? Your guess is as good as mine. I'm just much more focused on the end result than I am on all that boring prep work.

However, when it comes to parenting, my focus is all about the preparation. I employ prep-work tactics like prayer, communication, patience, observation, humor, and togetherness. Those tactics lay a solid groundwork so that when the paint splatters of life start flying, my children are well protected. I guess that's why my kids are turning out a lot better than my walls!

Years ago, when I was searching for ways to lead my children to make good decisions, I decided it would be far better to talk to them proactively about issues they would one day face than it would be to wait until they were buried under the consequences of their poor choices. I believed it would be easier to control the way they perceived the information and to help them understand the consequences of poor decisions if they could look at them objectively, without the added stress of peer pressure and other outside influences. I needed a safe way to talk with my kids about things like sex, drugs, alcohol, addictions, dating, pornography, Internet use, and other hot-button issues—perhaps even before they actually knew what those things were.

So, I devised a game I called Scenarios.

I would give my kids a scenario as though it were a situation they were facing at the moment. It ended with a choice they had to make between three or four options, which I spelled out to them. I made sure they felt safe in making any choice—even if it was clearly the wrong one. This was a learning exercise, and I much preferred that my kids make their mistakes within the safety of a dining room discussion rather than in another teenager's bedroom.

The practice of Scenarios became a favorite activity in my home and proved invaluable in preparing my teens to make good choices. The best parts were the talks we'd have after the choices were made and the consequences were presented. They felt free to explore, ask questions, experiment safely with the options—and then, when similar scenarios came up in real life, they were prepared to make the right choices.

The Hot Buttons series was birthed as a way for you to bring the principles and practices of my family's Scenarios game into your home. *Hot Buttons Dating Edition* deals with the boy-girl attractions and relationships that appear far too early in our kids' lives. You, as a parent, will glean information and practical tactics to employ in your home to immediately bring the issues that come with those relationships front and center.

In part 1, I will cover the idea of confronting hot-button issues in general—why, when, and how you should take a preemptive stand. Some parents may feel that ten or eleven years old is too young to start talking openly with tweens about things like date rape. These introductory chapters will explain why I vehemently disagree.

In part 2, I detail various hot-button issues to help you understand the specifics of what your teens or preteens face in boy-girl relationships these days. Each chapter of this section includes motivation, encouragement, and direction for setting boundaries, along with recommended action steps to take right away.

In part 3, I give you everything you need to start pressing the hot buttons and proactively preparing your teens to make good choices. You'll be able to take away practical and precise words in the form of *Strategic Scenarios* that will help you press the hot buttons that relate to dating. Your kids will be able to live out the scenarios and learn from their choices in a risk-free environment. I'll share truths about the topic, help you figure out how to handle it in your own home with the method of *Strategic Scenarios*, and give you a prayer you can pray to ask God to help you with that certain issue.

In part 4, you'll build relationship—relationship with God and with each other. You'll have the opportunity to identify specific dating hot buttons in your home, reverse mistakes, and do the work to repair any damage that may have already been done. Then you'll be prompted to make a plan to avoid those dangers in the future. You'll also be walked through the dual processes of confession and forgiveness, both within your family and in your relationship with God.

One thing you'll notice about each Hot Buttons book is that they're all structured in the same way. Some of the content is reiterated with subtle changes to direct it to the issue being discussed. This similarity is intentional. The truth of God's Word doesn't change, and the importance of good decisions is universal. The Bible is clear and effective—and speaks for itself. I recommend that you work through the parent-teen study guide for each book, even if you've done it before. The Lord will show you new things as you approach His Word for answers on each new hot-button issue.

Acknowledgments

I'm forever thankful to God for His gift of restoration. Considering all the mistakes I've made along the way, it's only by His hand of mercy that I have the life I do and the authority to write this book.

I need to thank fabulous authors Cara Putman, Jenny Jones, and Jill Williamson for taking the time to consider the premise of the Hot Buttons books and offer their professional endorsements.

My agent and friend, Chip MacGregor—you rock!

Thank you to my wonderful Twitter and Facebook friends for their endless help with my rapid-fire questions about dating.

I suppose a thank-you should go to my previous boyfriends—who shall remain nameless—for being unwitting research partners on the subject of dating.

Erik, Natalie, Emily, Logan, Megan, Ryleigh: my inspiration for life, love, and writing. My love for you guys is often too much for this mama's heart to take. I wish you could feel its depth for even a brief moment, but I guess it'll have to wait until you have kids of your own.

Wil, my wonderful husband, thank you for your undying support of what I do and for being such a great daddy. Even with all the bumps and bruises along the paths of our individual lives, I'm so glad we ended up together. I can't wait until we say, "Here we are, li'l ol' man and li'l ol' woman, sitting on a porch."

PART ONE

Dating
HOT
BUTTONS

What exactly is a hot-button issue? A *hot button* is any emotional or controversial issue that has the potential to trigger intense reaction. What topics jump to mind that fit this description when you think of teens and tweens? Pretty much everything that pummels your kids with temptation and threatens to pull them away from a walk with God. Music, dating, computer use, texting, partying . . . The list goes on. Moms and Dads, these issues are real and often confusing. They require attention—*before* they arise. Ignoring them can have dire consequences that our children will have to live with for the rest of their lives. The decision to just wait until an actual situation arises before we face a subject is naive, at best, and possibly lethal. We have both a parental right and a godly responsibility to hit these issues hard, head-on. If we approach them preemptively, our teens will be prepared to face and handle life's toughest battles.

Prepared:
Answering *Why*

If you're like me, watching a child transition into a dating teen is one of the scariest and most momentous periods to face as parents. I think many of us fear it because we still bear scars from our own foray into the world of adult relationships. We're all too fully aware that teenage dating relationships, and poor choices therein, can lead down a path of pain and destroyed hearts, and leave piles of devastated self-esteem in their wake.

But what do you do? Teens are going to have crushes; they're going to be attracted to and want attention from the opposite sex. You're powerless in the struggle. You should just pray hard, hold on, and hope the storm passes with little collateral damage, right?

Wrong.

Mom and Dad, you're in charge, and you need to set the rules. The teen years are an extremely important preparation time, and you need to stand up and make these years count. You don't need to *get* through these years; you need to *power* through them. Take charge, and make a difference.

Parents need to be in charge, but I'm not advocating for a take-no-prisoners attitude in our homes. Our children need to feel love, not condemnation. They should trust that we're an ally, not the enemy. In one sense, it's *us* against *them*. Us—our insight, our God-given wisdom, our life experiences—versus them—their temptations, their pressures, their desires. But you're not fighting against your kids in hopes of coming out victorious over them; you're in a battle *for* them.

> For our struggle is **not against flesh and blood**, but against the rulers, against the authorities, against the powers of this dark world and **against the spiritual forces of evil** in the heavenly realms. (Eph. 6:12)

Dispel the myth of effective insulation.

As Christian parents we try to insulate our families from negative outside influences. We keep watch over the things that enter their young minds through television, movies, and the like, and we keep them from participating in mature behavior like dating and relationships before they're ready. This is in no way intended to put them at a disadvantage but to shield them from the wiles of the enemy who whispers lies into their young, eager minds. It's not enough, however, to just say *no* (though that's a good first step).

We may wish we lived in a Christian bubble, able to insulate our children from the world, but pretending we do so ignores a huge need. It results in teens who are sent out into the world unarmed and unprepared for things they can't avoid. Our kids will face temptation, peer pressure, and sinful desires; it's a fact. It's more important to prepare your children than it is to attempt to create a sterile, sin-free environment in a world that makes it impossible.

Don't you wish we could walk with our kids through the battles of life—guarding and guiding them through each pressure-filled moment, each decision between right and wrong, each temptation? While God-honoring parents absolutely should have high expectations and maintain a tight grip on the reins as they raise their families, we also need to prepare our kids to stand alone.

Nothing we do can fully protect our kids from facing temptations, pressure-filled moments, decisions between right and wrong. You can't control what their peers throw at them, but you can affect how prepared they are to defend themselves against the onslaught. In each and every pressure-filled moment of decision, there comes a moment just before the final decision is made, a moment when all the preparation, forethought, and wisdom we've been equipping our kids with comes to a head. Once the hot button is pushed, the opportunity for laying groundwork is over. They know what they know, and in the heat of the moment there's no time for anything else. They make a choice based on all the work that came before. And our teens need to be equipped to make the right choice; armed with something more than *no*; braced by facts, your wisdom, and God's Word.

Teens will likely face persecution, disappointment, and even out-and-out rejection when they choose to stand for what's right, especially when it comes to their dating choices, and ultimately their purity (which is covered in *Hot Buttons Sexuality Edition*). If we're proactive, our children can reach their teen years empowered to make hard choices in the face of those afflictions—willing to withstand and endure them for the sake of Christ and for their own well-being.

Take the mystery out of sin!

In Mark 14:38, we're warned to watch and pray about temptation. Even for Christian adults, our spirits might be willing to avoid temptation, but we are cautioned to be attentive because our bodies are weak. How much more so for someone who isn't prepared for the temptation! We may have raised the most well-intentioned kids on the planet—ones whose spirits are willing—but their flesh is weak. They need to be trained.

> **Fix these words of mine in your hearts and minds**; tie them as symbols on your hands and bind them on your foreheads. **Teach them to your children**, talking about them when you sit at home and when you walk along the road, when you lie down and when you get up. (Deut. 11:18–19)

Before your kids approach dating age, you need to guide them in the knowledge and application of God's Word and the pursuit of His will. Ephesians 6:13 says, "Put on the full armor of God, so that when the day of evil comes, you may be able to stand your ground, and after you have done everything, to stand." (In chapter 10, we're going to do just that as it pertains to your teens and dating.)

As we move forward in fully equipping them, we need to teach them three things:

- Why it matters
- How to honor their commitments once they make them
- That they aren't alone

Why does it matter? What's in it for them if they stand on God's Word in the face of peer pressure, risking friendships, popularity, feel-good relationships? Our teens need to believe that the Lord has a plan for them and His ways are best. They need to care about arriving at the altar with their hearts intact. They need to see the value in preserving their sexuality and their purity. A time-invested parent, who prays as much as she talks and listens as much as she prays, will raise a child eager and willing to say NO and mean it.

How do they honor their commitments? Making commitments is scary. Preparing for the unknown is challenging. Teenagers need to make commitments with a clear mind and not wait until the pressure hits, but there's still the risk that they'll face a temptation and wonder why they ever made the promise in the first place. So, in order to keep those commitments, they need your continued guidance as they adapt to each new phase of life; and they need options—a busy life with wholesome things like church activities and sports, rather than too much time home alone plagued by boredom.

Where will we be during the process? Mom, Dad, Guardian—you need to make a commitment too. Your teen needs to know that you'll be aware of what's going on, and that you'll do whatever is needed to help them honor God, obey you, and respect themselves, including open the door to outside resources when necessary. This all requires time, communication, and godly insight into the minds of your teens. Our kids need to be a part of a family that is serving the Lord and watching parents who practice what they preach, so they can continuously grow in the knowledge of the Word and in relationship with God.

We can be confident parents, even in these scary times!

Today's choices can have permanent consequences for our children. It's difficult to let go and trust that everything will just work out fine in the end, knowing that some of our teens' decisions will affect the rest of their lives. When we recognize that they're ill-equipped to make those choices, it's very difficult not to panic. It would be easier to lock them up for a few years and check in at, oh, around twenty-two.

We do have a promise to cling to, though.

> **Being confident of this**, that he who began a good work in you will carry it on to completion **until the day of Christ Jesus**. (Phil. 1:6)

Let's break that down.

> *Being confident of this:*
> You can be sure that this is the way it is. It's a promise.

> *He who began:*
> Who began it? "He" did. Not you. Not your teen. God started . . .

A good work:
The work He started is a good and righteous thing.

Will carry it on to completion:
It will be finished. He didn't start something only to see it fall to pieces because of some teenage mistakes. It *will* be completed. It's a promise of God, and I choose to believe Him.

Until the day of Christ Jesus:
Here's the thing, though. Every one of us, including our teens, is a work in progress. This work, which will be completed, has a long way to go . . . until the day of Christ Jesus, to be exact.

The battle we fight in protecting, shielding, and preparing our teens for life's hot-button issues isn't as black-and-white as a physical battle in which the wins and losses can be easily quantified. We must often blindly face the battles for our kids, operating more on faith than on sight, being obedient to the call of Christ and reliant on the leading of the Holy Spirit. We have been given tools in God's Word to prepare us to guard against the confusion of this world, however. And we're granted partnership with the Holy Spirit, who will lead and guide us according to godly wisdom and sight. That guidance is invaluable as we prepare our kids for life's battles.

CHECK POINTS ➤➤➤

CHECK POINTS

✓ The battle we fight is not *against* our teens, it's *for* them!

✓ Knowing what's coming, we need to get in there and do some strategizing—some proverbial button-pushing—so we can prepare them for the spiritual war they're going to encounter.

✓ While God-honoring parents absolutely should have high expectations and maintain a tight grip on the reins as they raise their families, they also need to prepare their kids to face persecution, disappointment, and even out-and-out rejection when they choose to stand for what's right.

✓ It's more important to prepare your children than it is to attempt to create a sterile, sin-free environment in a world that makes it impossible.

✓ Our teens need to be equipped to make the right choice; armed with something more than *no*; braced by facts, your wisdom, and God's Word.

✓ Each pressure-filled moment of temptation, each decision between right and wrong, is backed up with some level of preparation—groundwork we've laid, conversations we've had, rules we've enforced.

Watchful:
Answering *When*

The days of Leave-It-to-Beaver style dating are over. When it comes to those all-encompassing boy-girl relationships, we don't have the luxury of waiting until a boy calls our daughter, assuming that will be her first signal that he's interested in her. We can't pretend that a no-dating-before-sixteen rule means there won't be anything going on in our son's love life that we're unaware of. In fact, these days, it's best to face facts fast.

Dating isn't a black-and-white sin issue. No one will say that going out to dinner is a sinful act. So the preparation for good decisions is going to take a lot of speculative work as you deal with the what-ifs. If you wait until the boy she's had a crush on for years starts talking to your daughter and flirting in school, or until that "hot" girl starts texting your son, it's going to be very difficult to pull a teenage head out of the clouds. The prep work must be done now . . . the sooner, the better.

What don't your kids want you to know?

Honestly, kids don't want you to know what *they* know or what *they* feel about sex, love, relationships, and attractions. They can't identify the tingles of temptation or the twinges of passion they're feeling, and they certainly don't want you to know about them. They don't want to admit that they're mentally exploring ideas and possibilities of the things they're discovering about themselves and others. They're afraid of what you'll think if you realize what's going on in their heads.

If you haven't already initiated conversations about the attraction of the opposite sex, it's highly unlikely that your teenager is going to run to you with her cell phone and show you a sexy message or picture she received, or that your son will show you the Facebook pictures of the girls who are flirting with him. But these kinds of secrets are when the erosion starts.

Those first flirts with danger, the first tempting sin—if it goes well— makes way for more and more. The only way to prevent that is with information and awareness.

How early is too early?

Since the world is throwing temptation and sin at your kids at incredibly young ages, you need to go after those tough issues even earlier than you think. (If you haven't heard the statistics yet, you're not going to believe them.) If your daughter is going be interested in boys in seventh grade, she needs to learn about her body and temptations and develop a plan for saying no while she's in sixth grade. If your son is going to like girls at fourteen, he needs to learn how to respect a girl and himself far earlier than that. If your child is going to be pressured to have sex in ninth grade, he or she needs to learn how to say no in eighth. Assuming your teens will make it through those stages unscathed without preparation is like push-ing them off a cliff, hoping they'll learn to fly before they hit the ground. Are you willing to take a chance that they won't fall headfirst?

You have to be willing to tackle tough issues openly and honestly be-fore they actually come up. That might feel uncomfortable—like you're giving your preteen or teenager too much information, too soon, and that it will give your kids ideas about trying those things. That can be espe-cially scary when it comes to dating and sexual subjects.

Let me ask you some questions:

- Do your kids show any interest in the opposite sex?
- Have your teens been out on a date?
- Have physical signs of puberty begun? If you're not sure, see chapter 4.
- Are your kids ever home alone?
- Are they ever at friends' houses where there's no supervision? Are you sure?
- Have they experienced a first kiss or participated in displays of affection like holding hands or hugging?

If you answered yes to any of those questions—even one—your concern shouldn't be whether it's too early to address this hot button but rather if it's *too late* for the kind of preemptive action I'm talking about. If you answered yes, then the chances are you need to begin taking a bit more of a *reactive* approach—which is equally necessary.

Don't misunderstand me. I'm not saying that all of those things in the list above are bad things, but they are open doors that expose your kids to issues you need to address. *Now*.

Just because you don't use swear words in your house, for example, you can't pretend your kids don't hear them on the school bus. My oldest daughter had learned all of them from the older kids on the bus long before it occurred to me that she might know them. You may shield your tweens from talk of dating and teen relationships, but what about the eleventh graders making out at the back of the bus? You might supervise kids at your home, but how can you be sure the parents of your children's friends monitor just as closely as you do?

If your teens have a good grasp on what God wants them to do with their hearts, if they grow in an understanding of what marriage is and how they want to enter that covenant one day, if they learn that the hurt associated with immature dating isn't worth it, they'll be well equipped to face dating decisions. In fact, they'll be likely to avoid situations where they even have to call upon the preparation; they just won't go there. The work you do now can save them from a lot of hurt and many, many mistakes; plus it paves the way to a successful marriage. Your grandkids will thank you one day.

How old is old enough?

Everyone is different. Some tweens are early bloomers and are far more advanced and aware than others of the same age. Then there are those who prefer to hang back in their innocence a little longer. In general, kids surrounded by older teens discover and experiment at a faster rate than those who are not.

Physical and emotional changes often go hand in hand, but not always at the same rate. There is a clear distinction between puberty and adolescence. *Puberty* is physical. The effects are ones we can witness as maturing bodies transform. These changes start at different times for each individual and span several years.

The changes of *adolescence*, however, are more emotional and mental. Even though the physical adjustments suggest that emotional changes are imminent, they don't always go right along the same path with the same speed. So it's the hidden, stealthy nuances that you need to watch out for.

Changes that signal adolescence:

> - dramatic change in behavior
> - separating or distancing from parents, other adults, and/or family members
> - showing more independence from Mom and Dad
> - wanting to fit in with peers
> - relying more on friends' opinions than parents'
> - experimenting with looks and identities
> - discarding childhood treasures, activities, and habits
> - blaming parents
> - being bored with family time, always looking for a way out of the house
> - lying or sneaking to talk to a boy/girl

What don't you want your kids to know?

Oh, believe me, I could make a list a mile long of the things I wish my teens didn't know about, and I'm sure you feel the same way. The problem is, your kids will know about all of those things at some point, if they don't already. You need to turn your thinking away from not wanting the knowledge to exist, and get it more focused on not wanting your teens to get curious and *explore* that knowledge on their own.

You don't want your teens to learn by personal experience:
- How the wrong choice feels
- How one mistake leads to another one
- The pain of the aftereffects
- The heartbreak
- The desire to undo something that can't be erased
- Regret

Can you save them from those things every single time?
- No, probably not.

Is saving them from one mistake worth all of this effort?
- Of course it is.

Let's stop being horrified by the truth about what our teens are faced with and start doing something to equip them to handle it. This book deals with various aspects of boy-girl relationships and all the potential dangers that accompany those relationships. Pretending boys and girls are not attracted to one another is like not talking about the elephant in the room. Eventually, that elephant is going to get restless and hungry. It's vital that you're educated about what your teens are thinking and feeling, armed with the tools to guide them, and then ready to stand watch.

CHECK POINTS

✓ Let's stop being horrified by the truth about what our teens are faced with and start doing something to equip them to handle it.

✓ Those first flirts with danger, the first tempting sin—if it goes well—makes way for more and more. The only way to prevent that is with information and awareness.

✓ Physical and emotional changes often go hand in hand, but not always at the same rate.

✓ Be educated about what your teens are thinking and feeling, be armed with the tools to guide them, and then be ready to stand watch.

✓ Turn your thinking away from not wanting the knowledge to exist, and get it more focused on not wanting your teens to get curious and *explore* that knowledge on their own.

✓ If your teens have a good grasp on what God wants them to do with their hearts, if they grow in an understanding of what marriage is and how they want to enter that covenant one day, if they learn that the hurt associated with immature dating isn't worth it, they'll be well equipped to face dating decisions.

Proactive:
Answering *How*

chapter 3

With adolescence on the horizon—or even in the rearview mirror—it's necessary to change your tactics. Childhood was a time of learning and discovery, a time when your child looked to you as the supreme teacher and guide. Now it's vital that you adjust your approach by encouraging open, honest, age-appropriate communication—even when the questions are difficult and demand tough answers. It's a challenge to make the transitions in accordance with their age, but it's necessary because, believe me, their friends are transitioning too, and along with those changes comes experimentation.

Whatever you do, don't *relate.*

You'll quickly lose credibility with your teens if you try to pretend you're like them. You're not. This isn't debatable. You're an adult with adult responsibilities, and you're at a place in your life when you're ready to face them. How can a teenager be expected to believe that you're a contemporary, a buddy, a friend? Furthermore, they don't want that or need that from you.

Studies have shown that teens feel the most distance from parents who try to be their friends. They have peers at school. At home, they need and want a parent.

This is especially true on the issue of boy-girl relationships. The quickest way to get your tween or teen to stop talking is for you to try to get her or him to open up under the guise of girl-talk or guy-talk. They will see right through that as being the ploy it is, and you will lose their trust. They want a parent, not a BFF.

Instead of trying to relate and be accepted by your teen as a contemporary, gain credibility by admitting and embracing your differences. Don't subject yourself to the eye roll and the comments about how out of touch you are; admit it yourself. Make it a source of humor between you and your teen. Embrace the generation gap as something to be proud of, not a deep, dark secret.

What Not to Wear

Make your teenager proud by dressing nicely and caring about your appearance. But don't take it so far that you're sharing clothes and trying to fit in with the teenagers. Be confident and stylish, but stay toward the middle of the pack. Trying to be too trendy is as glaring a faux pas as being frumpy and out of touch. Either extreme will be a source of embarrassment and a reason for your daughter or son to feel distanced from you.

Again, teenagers want to know their parents have a handle on life. If you're still floundering for your own identity and fighting to regain your youth, you're going to confuse your kids. Confidence, self-assuredness, and a moderate sense style will make you more of a cool yet dependable parent—a wardrobe straight out of your teen's closet will have the opposite effect.

What Not to Say

When you're talking to your teens and preteens about dating (or anything, for that matter), avoid trying to use teen-speak. It robs you of your credibility. My daughter says *uber* and *epic* all the time, but if I joke around and throw one of those words into a sentence, she just rolls her eyes. Why? Because she knows it's not me and that I'm just desperately and pathetically trying to relate to her on a level she doesn't need me or want me to. It's fake and contrived. Teenagers see right through that every single time.

Along with skipping those uberly epic phrases (see what I mean?), you want to think before you relate. Don't throw in a story from your past every time an issue arises. Wait until your teens ask you about your own teen years. A sure path to an eye roll is for you to say, "Oh, I went through the same thing when I was your age."

Avoid:
- ➤ "I can relate."
- ➤ "When I was your age . . ."
- ➤ "Oh, this will pass."
- ➤ "Wait until you have adult problems . . ."
- ➤ Trendy speech
- ➤ Saying that someone else has it worse—that feels impossible to your teen and seems like a brush-off.

- Trying to convince your son or daughter that this will go away—it's present now, that's all that matters.
- Belittling the issue—even though teenage problems aren't usually as big as adult problems, they are the most important thing to your teen in that moment.
- Laughing—this hardly needs commentary, but it happens so often. Don't tease your teens about their hormone-driven angst.

There are also some key validating phrases that can go a long way toward generally bridging the gap between you and your teen. (We'll get into specifics on the issues of dating in later chapters.)

"Wow. I can see why this would be a confusing situation for you."

"Ouch. That must hurt."

"Would you like advice, or want me to just listen?"

"That must be so frustrating."

Whatever you do, don't be unapproachable.

Mom, Dad, it's time to shoot straight. What happened the last time your teen approached you to have a chat? Did you even look up from your computer screen, television program, or book before you uttered one of those phrases your teens have learned to hate?

"Uh-huh."

"Sure, whatever."

"Not right now."

When asked what teens don't like about adults, the biggest complaint is that parents don't really listen. Teens feel dismissed, ignored. Below

I've listed some actual responses I received when I asked them that very question:

> "They pretend to hear by grunting, nodding, even sort of laughing when they think they should, but offer no real response to show me they even heard what I said."

> "They don't ask any questions about what I said. They're too happy I stopped talking and are afraid to 'put another quarter in' [a phrase that parent actually uses]."

> "Dad gets mad when I'm confused and just wants to spout out advice and expects me to take it without any further discussion."

> "They're 'too busy.'"

> "They say things like, 'Give me ten more minutes' or 'Not now, okay?' They aren't exactly rude, but they kind of brush me off."

> "I know my mom loves me, but I just wish I could have a little face time for real."

Ouch.

Before you're going to be able to make an impact regarding the hot-button issues in your teen's life, you're going to need to gain his trust. He must believe that you're interested in whatever interests him and cannot ever feel that you're bored by his concerns. And, much worse than feeling that you're bored is feeling that you're uninterested. If your teen feels like you just want him to go away, he will.

You and I know that whatever is bothering your teen will pass—maybe the next day or maybe next week. In a year, it will be a dim memory and other issues will have taken center stage. But more important than dealing with the specific issue or solving the immediate problem is to let your teen know that you take her seriously and care enough to listen to whatever it is. The feeling of rejection that comes when parents brush off concerns builds to an unidentifiable resentment that leads to rebellion and anger.

> > > **Challenge:** *The next time your kid walks in the room, close your laptop or turn away from the screen immediately. Or, if you're on the phone, end the call as soon as possible. Be available so it doesn't always have to feel like an interruption just to ask you a question.*

Whatever you do, don't preach.

If raising children were simple, parents would be able to share stories and offer advice, imparting the wisdom they gleaned from their own personal failures and poor decisions. The children would see their parents as interesting, protective, and wise. They would cling to the sage advice and suggestions their parent offered . . . in fact, they would beg for it.

But every parent knows that's just not the way it works. We didn't treat our parents that way, and our kids won't see us in that light either. Most preteens will pretend to listen just long enough to make Mom and Dad happy, and then blissfully and confidently go their own way, shucking the parental words off their shoulders with each step while they proceed to do whatever they want to do.

Like you and I did.

One of the most difficult things for parents and religious educators to do is to find a way to engage teenagers on a spiritual level over the table of Scripture. We believe wholeheartedly that God's Word, hidden in the hearts of believers, will guide them through life's tough choices and difficult moments. But until our kids have lived through pain and mistakes, until they've had a need to call on the Word of God themselves, it can be difficult to instill that dependency.

In other words, how do we get our teens to care about God's Word *now*, so they are armed and ready later when faced with hot-button issues? If we can't just wait and let our kids figure it out in their own timing, and we can't just tell them the way it is and leave it at that, then we need to find another way to get results.

Instead, speak truth with love and respect.

No matter how much you study or how passionate you are about the nuggets of truth you uncover in the Word, if you don't hand it down in love, it's meaningless. Scripture should never be used to attack, browbeat, or belittle. You should never, ever use Scripture to make your teen feel bad about herself or himself. You see, I've learned the hard way over the years that knowledge spewed without love just sounds hollow.

If I speak in the tongues of men or of angels, but do not have love, I am only a resounding gong or a clanging cymbal. If I have the gift of prophecy **and can fathom all mysteries** and all knowledge, and if I have a faith that can move mountains, **but do not have love, I am nothing**. (1 Cor. 13:1–2)

The knowledge of the *content* of the Bible without a grasp on the intent—the love—and without giving it the proper *context*, will never reach our kids. It cannot simply be a rule book. It's far too easy to rebel against rules. It must be a love letter. I can speak to teens about ancient customs and the true meaning of a Greek word until I fall over. But if I don't lovingly apply it in a way that makes sense to them, to their own lives, I've done nothing more than sound like a clanging bell that rings in their heads until the last dong fades into nothingness. I can be right, but that doesn't mean I'll get through to them.

It's not as easy as just handing down the facts and expecting our kids to soak them up like sponges. It simply doesn't work that way. Teens can tell if you've really taken the Scriptures to heart and applied them to your own life, or if you're just trying to do your parental duty by passing the doctrine on to them. They can tell if you're preaching out of control and fear, or if you're reaching out to them out of love and concern. Make sure the Bible is a part of each and every discussion you have about the choices your teens will make. That way, they'll understand that you're passing along God's Word, rather than coming at them with a because-I-said-so attitude.

Here are a few questions to ask yourself:

> ➢ Have you prayed over the topic before bringing it up to your teen?
> ➢ Are you taking biblical ideals and making them relevant issues for a teen?
> ➢ Are you using too many personal examples or lectures?
> ➢ Do your teens feel free to ask questions? Are you prepared to give or find an answer if they do?
> ➢ Are you offering application techniques, or just handing down rules?

In order to get them to care about God's Word, they need to feel nurtured, appreciated, and valued as a part of the body of Christ; they need to see themselves as an important group of Christians to which the Bible was also addressed. If we don't take the time to prayerfully pass down biblical truth and godly expectations in a modern way that appeals to our kids, then how can we fault them for not receiving it from us? Our babies come into the world fully trainable. We can't let go and expect them to teach themselves, because they will look for a source of education. It's your job to make sure you're the one providing it.

The truth is, human desires and the propensity toward sin haven't changed, but the accessibility of sinful things has definitely ramped up exponentially. Teens have access to alcohol, pornography, gambling, drugs, and sex in ways we never dreamed possible. We parents can't pretend that we have it all under control and that we can act as a shield to keep our teens from those things. Rather, we have to train them extensively, pray for them constantly, and bribe them occasionally. (Okay, I was kidding about that last part. Kind of.)

When it comes to dating, teens will often espouse as historical fact that teens got married in Bible times. Today's young people reason that if Bible-teens were ready to get *married* at fourteen, then surely today's fourteen-year-old is ready to at least *date*.

I offer a few responses to that argument:

1. You can't call upon age-old practices to make your case when they suit you, and then reject them as being out-of-date when they don't help your cause. Pick one way or another, and stick with it.

2. Those teens married because they were finished with education—such as it was—and ready to start a family. They didn't date for over a decade as people do today, as they weed through the possibilities. In fact, in those days, many couples didn't even meet until their wedding day.

3. Paul said it's better to marry than to burn with desire. True. But you won't need to "burn with desire" if you keep yourself out of situations charged with passion-potential.

If we can't just wait and let our teens figure out dating in their own timing, and we can't just "lay down the law" and leave it at that, then we need to find another way to reach them.

Instead, model by making right choices.

What were your dating years like? What mistakes did you make? Have you already resolved how you will answer the questions that will surely come? If you've made mistakes in your life—and come on, who hasn't?—are you living as a changed person, evidence of God's grace?

We can't ask our teenagers, who are far less prepared to deal with life's temptations than we are, to make good decisions if we're not modeling those right choices in front of them. How can we expect them to overlook our shortcomings and choose better for themselves if we don't show them what it means to be changed? Don't pretend to be perfect, just be honest about how you've been changed.

In 1 Corinthians 9, Paul writes to the church about this very topic. He warns against preaching the truth to others but living in such a way that you miss it yourself.

> Therefore **I do not run like someone running aimlessly**; I do not fight like a boxer beating the air. No, I strike a blow to my body and make it my slave so that after I have preached to others, **I myself will not be disqualified** for the prize. (vv. 26–27)

When things get tough, you'd better believe that they'll use your failures as excuses to justify their own. You can preempt that by being open about your past dating mistakes and sharing about what you wish you'd done differently. Don't pretend to be perfect, just be honest.

Let your teens know that living for Christ, defending truth, and standing up against sin aren't simple for you either. Relate to them with respect, and you'll get their respect back. Be open about the cost of doing the right thing so they'll know they're on the right path. Imagine if, when you were a teen, your parent had responded to a problem you were having by saying to you, "You know what? I struggle with that too. It's not easy for me to make the righteous choice when it comes to _____ either. I do it because I know it's best for me and because I know God chose that as the way for me to walk, so I do my best to walk in it." How would this have made you feel? Would you have responded with the "dreaded eye roll"?

It helps teenagers when they can see their parents as human beings with weaknesses, failures, and struggles. They don't feel so alone in the struggle when they see the need we all have for the grace of God and the power of the Holy Spirit in battling sin.

Instead, provide "real life" practice.

Unfortunately, the best way young people learn is through personal experience. But we don't want to wait until they make the mistakes in order for them to learn from their mistakes. So, what can we do?

This is where these Hot Buttons books come in. When we use the Strategic Scenarios, purposeful dialogue about hot-button dating issues will provide us the opportunity to sneak in something resembling personal experience for our kids—without the dreaded ramifications—while also teaching them that their opinions, thoughts, and feelings are important and valid.

CHECK POINTS ➤➤➤

CHECK POINTS

✓ It's a challenge to make transitions in accordance with kids' ages, but it's necessary because their friends are transitioning too, and along with those changes comes experimentation.

✓ Teens can tell if you have really taken the Scriptures to heart and applied them to your own life, or if you're just trying to do your parental duty by passing them on.

✓ Without giving it the proper *context*, knowledge of the *content* of the Bible will never reach our teens.

✓ If I don't lovingly apply Scripture in a way that makes sense to my kids, I've done nothing more than sound like a clanging bell.

✓ Human desires and the propensity toward sin haven't changed, but the accessibility of sinful things has ramped up exponentially.

✓ Don't pretend to be perfect, just be honest about how you've been changed.

✓ Let your teens know that living for Christ, defending truth, and standing up against sin aren't simple for you either.

✓ Unfortunately, young people learn best through personal experience. This is where Strategic Scenarios come in.

PART TWO

Identifying the Dating HOT BUTTONS

Long ago, dating was so much more casual than it is today. That might sound bad, but it wasn't. Dating was fun, cute, simple. Girls waited for boys to call them. They got dressed up and went for a burger and a coke on a Friday night. They were home by ten o'clock and no good boy would risk breaking curfew or being inappropriate with a girl, and no good girl would want a boy who did.

All that has changed. Dating is barely even the point anymore. Boys and girls either jump in and out of one serious relationship after another, or they don't commit to anyone and have sex with everyone. Parents are busy and they're just wading through the teen years hoping to get to the other side. So teens, left to figure out relationships with the opposite sex on their own, take the path of least resistance and follow the crowd.

Can we return to days gone by and instill an expectation of purity in our teens? What can we do or say to unearth a godly patience in them that desires growth and maturity over pleasure and short-term gratification? If we identify the specific hot buttons associated with dating, we can address them more easily and effectively. Armed with specific information, we'll best be able to get our tweens and teens ready to make good choices.

Early Boy-Girl
Relationships

One of my triplets' favorite movies is *Toy Story 3*. What an amazing digital feat as well as a compelling story with appeal to all ages! My kids could watch it over and over—and they have. There's a scene in the first half of the movie that takes place in Sunnyside Daycare when Ken and Barbie meet for the very first time. Ken stops talking mid-sentence, and they both stop dead in their tracks (as much as Mattel toys can be dead). They gaze into each other's eyes as *Dream Weaver* begins to play in the background.

Every single time we get to that moment in the movie, my two-year-old son, Logan, gasps, covers his mouth with his chubby little hands, and whips his head around to look at me with wide eyes and then looks back at the screen. He bounces on his seat and grins until the scene ends. He understands that something special happened there in that moment. Something within him instinctively responds to the attraction and connection between Barbie and Ken. Interesting to note, he reacts to it far differently than his same-age siblings who barely even seem to take notice of that scene.

What's perceived as normal?

The toddler and preschool years are nothing but a hotbed of awareness. Whatever your young children witness about relationships—either what you model or what they see on television—is the foundation they'll build upon when they grow into relationships of their own. It's vital to be intentional about what is portrayed to them. For example, if you're a single parent who jumps in and out of dating relationships and parades those in front of your preschooler, how many dating partners do you think she or he will have in high school? Or, if you're in a volatile marriage with a lot of fighting and belittling, how do you think your son will treat girls and your daughter will allow herself to be treated? Preschoolers don't have the framework to question what they're witnessing, so it's absorbed as natural, therefore becoming their framework by default.

Second, third, and fourth graders are pairing up in fulfillment of what they interpret to be their culturally expected boy-girl role. Many think it's a rite of passage and are eager to fall in line with the crowd. Phone calls, passing notes, "going out"—those are all very real activities in elementary school. And girls make just as many calls or initiate just as many texts as boys—in fact more, from what I've seen in my daughters' friends. By the way, when I asked young people today what it meant to them to say they were "going out" with a boy or girl, they all said a similar thing: "It's not like we're going anywhere, it just means we're together." They're designating themselves as paired up. In a relationship. Exclusive.

The relationship itself is usually perfectly innocent at this stage, but kids are unprepared for the related fallout: when they argue with a friend over a crush, when they get "dumped" and feel rejected, when they like someone who doesn't like them back. They aren't emotionally or mentally ready to handle being focused on even a healthy relationship, so they definitely aren't prepared to handle the negative aspects of one.

Are we foolish enough to think that elementary school students won't advance their relationships as they themselves mature? That they won't get bored with the passing of "Do you like me? Circle Yes/No" notes? Naturally, these pairings become more sophisticated as the years pass and as puberty sets in with a vengeance.

Ready or not? Not.

Instead of thrusting them into the world of childhood relationships, we should be spending those early years teaching and modeling godly ways to treat the opposite sex. Boys must be shown how to honor and respect girls, how to uphold and cherish their virtue, and how to help them build upon it. Girls need to be shown patience and self-respect. They need to learn to wait for the right time, to value themselves for the right reasons, and not to manipulate boys.

These years need to be spent teaching that a love relationship is something for later. Something to get ready for. Something to help them prepare for marriage, not something to jump in and out of for decades until a random wedding occurs just because the timing seems right. And we wonder why the divorce rate is moving above 50 percent. We need to teach that people are not possessions to be traded throughout all of life. Instead, they are gifts, to be received at the right time—God's time.

It's a natural part of life. Can't I just leave the if and when questions of dating up to my child? An elementary-aged child? A fourth or fifth grader? What? . . . Are you crazy?

I react that way, not to insult your intelligence, because I believe you have the very best of intentions for your kids (after all, you're taking the time to read these books) and would go to great lengths to assure their spiritual, physical, and emotional well-being. So allow me to be frank here: it is a bold-faced lie of Satan that your elementary school-aged children will *inevitably* pair off in relationships, attractions, elementary school going out . . . whatever. By making you believe that lie, his hope is you'll help fulfill it.

NO. NO. NO.

I didn't allow young boy-girl relationships with my older kids, and won't with my littles. Many of my friends didn't or don't allow it either. But many, many have. Care to guess which ones call me with heartache as their kids make adult decisions with their teenage bodies? Guess which one called to tell me of her sixteen-year-old daughter's pregnancy. You see, their teens were far too advanced when it came time to date because the physical and emotional progression had been going on for years and years.

At this stage (and even later), friendships are good. Encourage your kids to be friends with boys and girls alike. Encourage innocence and honesty. Forbid the designation of any kind of pairing or relationship. If you don't, you're relinquishing power now, and you'll find it's nearly impossible to gain it back.

What if it's too late? Ah, I figured this would come up. Many of you are past the point I described above and fear it might be too late. Your teens have been on the road of physical attraction and dating for a while now. You left it up to them, and now you want to take the power back. Right?

Yeah, it's going to be difficult, but it can—and must—be done.

Immediately evaluate, for the purpose of change, your
> Communication
> Rules and expectations
> Consequences and follow-through
> Lifestyle

Action Steps

Whether responding to the issues of dating and relationships proactively or reactively, you need to take some steps immediately to set standards and construct boundaries. It's going to take work and a commitment to following through with the ongoing guidance needed.

1. Evaluate your communication style. If you're "friends" with your teen, make an about-face and take on the language and attitude of an authoritative figure. I'm not advocating a drill sergeant approach by any means, but this is the first thing that must change. For example, if you want your teenager to do more homework and say, "I wish you'd turn off that music when you study," you'll likely get a response like, "I think better with it on." Then the door closes in your face and the music is turned up to deafening levels. You don't "wish" for things, you require them. "You're studying right now, please turn the music off." It's not a suggestion.

If one of my kids said, "I think better with it on," and shut the door in my face only to turn the music up louder (which they would never do), I would respond by opening the door and permanently removing the stereo, along with any other electronic distractions. I might even take the door off its hinges for a time. Overreaction? Some might think so, but it's the knowledge that I *would* react that way that keeps my kids from treating me like that. Shutting a door in my face? No way. Mom and Dad, if you're allowing that level of disrespect, you're being walked all over, and you must take charge.

2. Evaluate your rules and expectations. Are you too lenient? This must be evaluated honestly. Make a list of the main rules in your home, dating and otherwise, and consider which of them were stretched by compromise—compromise made for the sake of keeping the peace. If you find that you've allowed your expectations to be tailored by your teen's whines and demands, you've allowed your child to claim the power, and you must take it back.

Are you in the habit of giving in too easily? From the time my kids were all teeny, tiny babies, I had them sleeping through the night by simple consistency. My preemie triplets slept twelve hours a night by the time they were five months old. This is because I reacted the exact same loving way each and every time they demanded my attention. I lavished my love and constant attention on them by day and then parsed it out on my terms at night. After only a few days, they realized that the night was different than the day and that the reward of getting me into their room wasn't worth the effort, so they just went back to sleep.

Teenagers are human beings too. If they can depend on you giving in after thirty minutes of arguing and door slamming, you'd better believe they'll push it to that point. But if they come to realize that you're never going to give in to any amount of arguing, and that, on the contrary, a bad attitude will only make things worse for them, eventually they'll tire of the fruitless battle of wills.

The Holy Spirit is tugging at your heart to set boundaries that are ordained by God. Satan is tugging at your teen to rebel against them. Don't let him win, and in doing so, lead your teen away from God.

3. *Evaluate your consequences and follow-through.* Consequences exist throughout all of life. Teenagers think they're immune. They work really hard to create an environment free from punishment and discipline by making it hard on Mom and Dad when consequences need to be exacted.

Do the hard thing and make them pay the predetermined price for their actions. Show your kids that you're willing to go into battle, that their life lessons are more important to you than anything else you have going on. Make it swift and costly.

4. *Evaluate your lifestyle.* Sorry, but this is a big one. Do you lead a disciplined, respect-worthy lifestyle? Do your kids look at you as someone they wish to emulate one day? Can they honestly say that you're putting the family first and living for God? If not, something needs to change.

Another thing to look at is the kind of relationship modeling you're doing. Are you living in a way that will convince your teens that purity is the very best option? Are they seeing you exist in a loving, healthy relationship that proves it's worth the wait? If you're a single parent, are you modeling the standards you're asking of your teen? If not, it's time to get a handle on that. Seek forgiveness for your mistakes, and plot a course for pure living that honors God and the beauty of patience and a righteous marriage.

Heavenly Father, thank You for entrusting me with the lives of these precious little ones. Please help me to be the parent You've called me to be—willing to do the difficult things in Your name, in order to raise godly people. Help me to guard my children from entering the world of boy-girl attractions and dating too early. Please give me wisdom to see what's happening right in front of me so I can intervene where I need to, and give me the guts to say no, even if it goes against the grain. I just want the best for my kids, and I know You have the best plan for them already mapped out. Help me to see it. Amen.

CHECK POINTS ▶▶▶

CHECK POINTS

✓ The stage for your kids' future outlook on relationships is being set in those early toddler and childhood years, so it's vital to be intentional about what is portrayed to them.

✓ Preschoolers don't have the framework to question what they're witnessing, so it's absorbed as natural, therefore becoming their framework by default.

✓ Children aren't emotionally or mentally ready to handle being focused on even a healthy relationship, so they definitely aren't prepared to handle the negative aspects of one.

✓ Instead of thrusting them into the world of childhood relationships, we should be spending these early years teaching and modeling godly ways to treat the opposite sex.

✓ It is a bold-faced lie of Satan that your elementary school-aged children will inevitably pair off in relationships, attractions, "going out". . . whatever. No. No. No.

✓ If you find that you've allowed your expectations to be tailored by your teen's whines and demands, you've allowed your child to claim the power, and you must take it back.

✓ Encourage innocence and honesty. Forbid the designation of any kind o' pairing or relationship. If you don't, you're relinquishing power now, and you'll find it's nearly impossible to gain it back.

chapter 5

To Date or Not to Date?

I overheard a twelve-year-old girl tell my daughter that she'd been out on a date with her boyfriend the night before. I had to pry my jaw from the ground before I jumped into the conversation. I wanted to confirm what I suspected—that it was a family outing and the boy was allowed to join them. Nope. She assured me that she and her also twelve-year-old boyfriend were driven to the mall and dropped off, where they had dinner in the food court, wandered around for an hour, and then went to a movie. They were picked up after four hours alone.

I asked my daughter about it later, and she confirmed this to be very common among many of her friends. She said the proverbial words: "Everybody does it," but followed them with, "Well, not me. And I don't want to." *Phew.*

My intention has always been to do as my parents did and not let my kids date until they were sixteen, hoping they'd choose to wait even longer. But I suddenly had to face the fact that I wasn't reading the situation clearly enough—I had blinders on.

You see, I had already realized long ago kids that age got into boyfriend-girlfriend pairs, and I knew from my own experiences that teens sneak around to do what they want to do. But I didn't realize how common it was for parents to actually allow and even encourage preteens to go out on single dates without any supervision, or even be in the home alone with no chaperone. This astounded me—someone who often gets asked for advice on ways to help teens stay pure. Well, I'd start right here with my advice:

Supervise.

Everything.

Constantly.

Yes, it's normal for a preteen to be interested in the opposite sex.

While some teens tend to be interested in dating earlier than others, it's a normal and very common adolescent stage to put rock-star posters on the wall and fawn over a television star. They do that because it's safe, but if that boy actually walked into the room, they'd have no idea how to handle themselves. Subconsciously, they know they're not ready.

They play like that for a little while, until they think they're ready for the real thing. Then, when the time feels right, girls usually pursue the relationship idea before boys do, who take their cues from the girls their age. In all but a few rare cases, left to his or her own desires, your teenager is going to want to date at some point or another. Usually sooner, rather than later.

But their desire or expectation doesn't necessarily mean they should be allowed to date. This doesn't have to be a compromise you make with your teen or something you just have to accept as a rite of passage. You need to think and pray about the standards and rules you want to set in your home and make them clear to your preteen long before the hormones hit. Be the parent, not the victim of circumstances you think you can't control. It takes intentional, purposed training with a lot of forethought and communication to raise a teen who can recognize the value in waiting.

> A recent survey suggested that if a child has a first date between the ages of 11 and 13, he or she has a 90 percent probability of being sexually active during senior year in high school. First date at age 14 leads to a 50 percent chance; first date at age 16, 20 percent chance.[1]

If kids start dating earlier and earlier (like twelve in the case of my daughter's friend) but get married later and later (late twenties to early thirties after achieving advanced degrees, rather than mid-teens like in Bible times), then they're subjecting themselves to decades of heartbreak. When it does come time to marry the love of her life, what does your daughter have left to offer him? How many cycles of love and heartbreak will your son have endured and/or caused by that time?

What's the point of dating?

Dating means more to the participants than just a chance to hang out together. If it didn't, they wouldn't fight so hard to be able to do it, and it would mean just as much to hang out with their same-sex friends. It's the attitude of connection, surrender, and partnership that they crave.

Dating, by the world's standards, is a period in life where you get to try out many people until you get lucky enough to find one you want to be with—at least for a while. This can only end with broken hearts, bad memories, and damaged intimacy for the future. (For more on this, see *Hot Buttons Sexuality Edition*.) By allowing this method of trial and error, we're raising another generation of people looking to others—rather than to God—to find someone who completes them.

Connecting with members of the opposite sex is not a teen's rite of passage; it's not something that every teen does; it's not unavoidable. These same things society says are natural experiences cause heartache and lead to sexual experimentation. How can that be God's plan for our teens?

Children, tweens, and teens are, by nature and design, selfish individuals, as is every human being without the proper training. So, with that selfishness in mind, what is the motivation in the person who wants to date your teen? And what is your child's motivation? God would have us raise well-adjusted confident teens who look to Him—not a boyfriend or girlfriend—for acceptance, assurance, self-worth.

How do I decide when (or if) to allow dating?

In most households, the subject of dating will come up at some point—hopefully later rather than sooner. So, instead of setting a rule about an age requirement, you can take inventory on a regular basis to determine the readiness of your teen. It's okay to make this an individual thing; you aren't required to set the same exact rules for every kid in your household. Until you feel that the following character strengths are in place, I'd recommend holding off on allowing dating.

1. *Exhibits some level of maturity.* You know that things change with growth. The things you once appreciated in other people might be complete turn-offs to you now. It will be the same for your teens, so don't create a playing field where your teens try out all sorts of different people just because they can—just because you let them. They should wait until they're prepared to know what they're looking for in a relationship and future spouse.

2. *Demonstrates the ability to resist temptation.* The younger the couple, the more difficult it is to fend off physical temptations and lustful feelings because they can't fully understand the lifelong ramifications of their actions. Take it from Paul, who said: "Flee . . . youthful lusts" (2 Tim. 2:22 NKJV). The sin isn't the lust itself; it's the inability to flee from the heated moment that leads to sin.

3. *Differentiates between* like, lust, *and* love. How many elementary school relationships (or even high school relationships) did you have that lasted forever? So, were they true, lasting, forever love relationships? No, of course not. True love doesn't wear out or run away. It's a God-given part of a human soul, not a hormone-driven, backseat moment of unbridled passion. Help your teens wait for true love by teaching them the difference.

4. *Makes wise selections.* Pay very close attention to the types of people who attract your teens. Is your daughter mostly interested in the bad-boy types? Is your son interested in the girls who seem the most

provocative? These types of people are not only poor choices for early relationships, but they signal that your teen's priorities and focus may be out of sync with God's. It's true that you can't judge a book by its cover, but you can definitely get an idea of the message its author is trying to send.

5. *Takes responsibility and accepts consequences for actions.* Adult behaviors result in adult consequences. Is your teen ready to take responsibility for whatever happens? Obviously this can apply to sex, pregnancy, and the like. But it also applies to matters of the heart. Emotional surrender to another person is an adult choice and carries the weight of adult pain.

So, what am I saying? That teens can't go to a movie together anymore? That they can't go out for burgers and fries after a football game? No. Not at all. Just remember that times have changed. There is nothing new under the sun as far as temptation and sin, but the disparity between the age society throws adult choices at our teens and the age at which they're actually ready to handle them is so great, we need to step in and help our kids be kids.

How can you know if your teen meets those standards outlined above?
- Ask questions.
- Then listen.
- Talk openly and regularly.

Some questions you can ask:
- ➤ Why do you want to date?
- ➤ What do you hope to accomplish by dating?
- ➤ How do you feel about the boundaries we've instilled?
- ➤ What makes it easy and what makes it difficult to be strong?
- ➤ What are your plans for dealing with pressure?
- ➤ What do you think about the dating habits of your friends?
- ➤ What are your plans for dealing with temptation?
- ➤ How can I help you?

Then what?
- ➤ Ask again. *Soon.* So you can stay on top of, and react to, any shifts in thinking.

How much privacy should I allow?

Parents are rarely comfortable not knowing what is going on in their child's life. It's hard to see a teenager walk out the door and take off with a date, hoping they'll remember what they've been taught, unable to monitor their every move. When that time comes, pray with them and pray for them. Trust that you've done the best you could and ask the Lord to be with them every step of the way.

I am urging you, parents:

Allow no complete privacy.

I'm not suggesting that you need to sit between your teen and his date at the movie theater, but there should never be a moment when they are alone without an adult in the house. Often parents lighten that control as teens get older, but the older they get, the more important it is to protect them from themselves.

It's not a matter of trust.

I'm not saying specifically that your teens are too weak to withstand pressure or temptation. How could I know that? But similarly, how can you be sure they aren't? It's far better to create an environment of power and self-control, where they have you to rely on, than to leave them to their own devices. They will thank you one day.

What if my teen is "in love"?

How do I know if I'm in love? When teens ask that question, parents often make the mistake of quipping back with, "You're too young for love!" While that is probably true, its dismissiveness does nothing but turn your teen off to everything you say next. Teenagers think the sun rises and sets around their current love interest. Those stirrings are very real to them, and they like the way they feel so much, they're willing to push you away in favor of nurturing that romance.

Validating their feelings sets a foundation for future conversations and mutual respect on this subject: "I understand what it feels like to care about someone like that." Notice, that statement didn't say *love*, and it didn't allow for any future potential; it simply said, "Yeah, I get it."

Next, you want to help them understand what they're feeling and make good decisions. Ask questions; teens love to talk about how they feel if they believe they're being heard and not judged. "How long have you felt this way?" "What do you like most about _____?" And so on.

The Three L's

Validate what they're feeling by helping them learn the difference between *like, lust,* and *love.*

Like: You have fun together. You're attracted to each other and you get butterflies around each other. You think about each other all the time.

Lust: All of the above plus the added dimension of sexual desire.

Love: You want to join your life and become one with this person. You could see raising a family together, and you're willing to work through problems.

The butterflies of like and the tingle of sexual desire do not add up to the commitment of love. It's very important they understand that and protect those three little words: *I love you.* More on that in upcoming chapters.

Action Steps

- Start dialogue about dating right away.
- Work through the Strategic Scenarios in chapter 11.
- Set standards and rules for dating in your household.
- Make the entire family aware of them before the time comes.
- Create a dating contract.

- Create a rescue scenario. Agree to pick up your child no matter what or where if the need arises.
- Be open and willing to talk about anything—validate feelings.
- When it's time for dating relationships, allow group dates or supervised activities.
- No closed doors—in your home or others.
- Confirm that parents at the homes of your teens' friends have the same values or are at least willing to uphold yours.
- Teach self-worth.

Above all else, **guard your heart**, for everything you do flows from it. (Prov. 4:23)

Father, I lift up my kids and their future spouses to you right now. Please place a hedge of protection around them and help them stay focused on the prize. Help them withstand the pressures of dating, relationships, and sex that they may unite as one, pure before You, on their wedding day. Help me guide my kids to have a long-term perspective rather than to seek short-term satisfaction. Show me what I need to see and give me the right questions to ask. Please help me reach my kids in ways most parents aren't able. Show them that waiting is good and right. Amen.

CHECK POINTS ➤➤➤

CHECK POINTS

✓ Dating doesn't have to be a compromise or something you just have to accept as a rite of passage in your teen's life. You need to think and pray about the standards and rules you want to set and make them clear to your preteen long before the hormones hit.

✓ Be the parent, not the victim of circumstances you think you can't control. It takes intentional, purposed training with a lot of forethought and communication to raise a teen who can recognize the value in waiting.

✓ Validate what they're feeling by helping them learn the difference between *like*, *lust*, and *love*.

✓ When that time comes, pray with them and pray for them—trust that you've done the best you could and ask the Lord to be with them every step of the way.

✓ The disparity between the age society throws adult choices at our teens and the age at which they're actually ready to handle them is so great, we need to step in and help our kids be kids.

✓ It's better to create an environment of trust, where teens are in control of themselves but have you to fall back on, than to leave them to their own devices, searching and confused.

Missionary
Dating

You want nothing more than for your teens to serve God whole-heartedly and live their lives as though missionaries, bringing God's love to wherever they are serving Him at the moment—school, a job, church, everywhere. You believe in the great commission to go and make disciples. You've taught your teens to be zealous in sharing the gospel with unbelievers. You've even encouraged friendships with non-Christians because you know that's what Jesus would have done.

Then one day, your sixteen-year-old daughter tells you that she has fallen for a boy from an atheist family. Not only was he not brought up in church and doesn't have a relationship with the Lord, but the kid was raised to actively oppose Him. What do you do? Forbid the relationship? Your daughter reminds you that you want her to be a zealous witness and that Jesus loves this boy, too. She admits that she prays God will reach him through her.

She's embarking on the path of missionary dating—entering a relationship with someone with the hope of introducing him to God and bringing him along in the faith. She assures you that she's strong enough to handle it and has a special burden for him.

What do you do?

Or, how about your son who wants to date a seeking unbeliever? She's searching for truth and open to it, but hasn't quite made the step toward a commitment to Christ. He assures you that she is open to his faith and will support it while she searches for her own answers. He promises not to push her but admits to feeling desperate to introduce her to his Savior, Jesus. He believes that by joining in a boyfriend–girlfriend relationship with her, he'll be in a better position to achieve that goal. Plus, he really digs her.

What do you do?

Think about the teaching in 2 Corinthians 6:14: "Do not be yoked together with unbelievers . . ." Did you know that verse isn't specifically referring to dating, or even marriage? It's talking about how believers shouldn't put themselves in any connection or a partnership where they are dependent upon the leading or even agreement of an unbeliever. Imagine two farm animals—oxen usually—yoked together by a wooden piece over their shoulders that attaches to the plow. They have to be the same kind of animal and even of similar size, strength, and temperament in order to do the job they need to do. Equal in those things, united by the yoke, they work together to achieve the work their master wants them to do.

Even though the context of the verses doesn't discuss marriage, the principle is still sound. After all, marriage is *work*! How could a believer who is surrendered to Christ for guidance and strength accept direction from and share decision-making power with someone who doesn't serve the same master? The motivation and the goal are unbalanced, to say the least; it always puts the believer in a position where compromise on the grounds of keeping the peace in the relationship seems prudent. A Christian will never be happy or fulfilled if tethered to someone who constantly pulls in the direction opposite the believer's passionate pursuit of Christ.

Make the hard choices.

When I finally began the painstakingly slow process of getting myself right with the Lord after taking a walk away from Him for a time, everything I had going on in my life was subject to scrutiny. At the time, my young son, Erik, and I were living with someone I loved very much. This man was one of the nicest people I'd ever met, and everyone loved him. The problem was, he didn't believe in God. He wasn't opposed to me going to church or whatever I needed to do, but he had never felt a need for God, himself. Everything in his life had gone pretty well; he had a lot of friends, and was a respected and happy person without any help from God—as he saw it.

One day, I found out he had purchased a ring and was about to ask me to marry him. I panicked.

Facing the prospect of marriage to an unbeliever, I had some tough choices to make. I really wasn't living for the Lord myself, but I knew enough about Him that I fully expected to be drawn back into fellowship with Him very soon. I knew the signs and understood that the convictions I was feeling were from the Holy Spirit. I feared I would make a mistake, marry this man, and have a lifelong tug between the call of God and my love for my husband. Those two things are powerful when they work together, but devastating when they oppose each other.

I ended it.

Oh, it was hard. I remember the conversation clearly. He was stunned. I was stunned. But more than being in shock, I felt release. I felt the tension oozing out of me like the steam from a pressure cooker. The part of my heart that was committed to God began to waken and I knew beyond a shadow of a doubt I'd done the right thing.

It still wasn't easy. I almost changed my mind several times. But I stayed my resolve and moved across the country with my little boy—back home with Mom and Dad.

I remember going bowling with a friend a few days after I moved home. Erik was around two and obviously didn't grasp the concept of the game. He took off running out onto the lane. I saw bowling balls whizzing by as he approached one of the gutters, so I sprinted out onto the lane to retrieve him—not thinking about the oil they use to slick the surface to make the balls fly faster.

Wham! My feet flew out from under me and I landed on my back, staring up at the goofy, '70s disco lights. I lost it right there. I started to cry. Then bawl. Then weep. I was homeless. Jobless. Alone. A failure. I felt broken by the mistakes I'd made, humiliated at the mess I'd made of my life, and hopeless at the prospects of my future. That fall to my back was the final straw, but it was a turning point for me. It was the bottom of my pit, and right then and there I turned it all over to God. I let go.

Everything changed after that. One of the first things I noticed was that my reasons for doing things had changed. My choice to end the relationship was because I was motivated by the beginning stirrings of what would become a deep love for God and a desire to please Him—deeper even than my own temporary situation or desires; but I still wanted control. Over time, as I drew closer to God following that bowling-alley conversion, He revealed His heart to me, and I began to really discover why He prompted me to make the choice I made.

Over the years, I've talked with and counseled a lot of women who are married to unbelievers. The agony they suffer by being pulled in opposite directions, even by very loving and tolerant spouses, is palpable. I don't believe they are able to live their Christian walk to its fullest potential, and I also believe their marriage inevitably suffers over the division. It's second best in every way and not at all what God designed.

Please, please, if you are in a marriage that is unequally yoked, don't become discouraged by my words. I pray that your marriage will flourish, and you'll both come to share in a walk with God. Realize that my goal here is not to tear you down for your choices but rather to save young people from making a mistake. And the preparation to avoid tragic mistakes in marriage must start in the pre-dating years.

Avoid the mind-set of compromise.

I've already pointed out that the vast majority of preadult relationships don't last anyway, so what's the big deal? Why can't kids date nice kids, even if they're not Christians? As long as parents are supervising them, why do they have to be believers? They're just kids. They're just having fun. It's not really any different from them having same-sex friends who aren't Christians. It's not like they're getting married or anything, right?

Again, wrong, wrong, wrong.

Come on, parents, you know this: early choices establish later patterns. And, eventually, your son or daughter will date the person they're going to marry. Parents who allow their children to date anyone—the boy next door whom she's known all her life, the girl from youth group who only wears black, that nice Muslim boy—are tacitly agreeing that it's okay for their child to have a relationship (which could lead to marriage) with that person. And of course, the potential for negative peer pressure also ramps up when the kids don't have families that share the same convictions (her mom may provide her with birth control, for instance; he might be allowed to see R-rated movies).

Think about a marriage relationship with a believing wife and an unbelieving husband. The unequally yoked believer must compromise her faith in order to keep the marriage relationship peaceful. She can no longer serve God in the way He's called her to—free, open, vibrant—without worrying about how it makes her unbelieving husband feel. When that compromise begins, her walk with God becomes undernourished and weak. Eventually, her guilt about the compromise will drive an even deeper wedge between them than the one that already existed.

Over time, she finds they can't share in life's greatest passion. He doesn't support or enjoy her greatest pleasures, and she can't abide his attachment to the world. Dates and time spent together become compromises for both of them. Eventually, they each feel bitterness at not being able to live out their desires and find true happiness. Resentment starts to take root, and the couple pulls away from each other.

The easy question here is: Why? Why let that happen? Early on in the dating years, set the standard that your teens may only date those who share the same level of faith in God, so they will edify and strengthen spiritual growth in each other, not chip away at it or prevent it entirely.

Prohibit anything less for your kids.

It's really that easy.

Be ready to answer opposition.

"But, even Jesus hung out with unbelievers!"

Your response: You bet He did! And you should too. Hanging out, associating, befriending, loving . . . those things are all very different from uniting, binding, and covenanting. A believer is called to that level of connection. And a believer can fulfill that calling in an even deeper way when he's joined with a partner who shares in it.

"What if I'm the only way he'll find God?"

Your response: Easy one! Is God so powerless that He would require you to sacrifice your walk with Him and become unequally yoked? Is He unable to draw someone to Himself without your help? No way. No human relationship is worth sacrificing your relationship with God.

"I'm strong enough not to let myself get pulled down."

Your response: Imagine standing on a chair with me on the floor in front of you. Reach your hand down, and pull me up to the chair. It's impossible, right? Now, if I pull on your hand, you immediately fall to the ground at my feet. It's far easier to be pulled down yourself than it is to pull someone up to your level.

Action Steps

As you continue to read through this book, you'll be led to employ what I call Strategic Scenarios to help train your teens on the subject of dating, and to teach the importance of choosing the right people to date. That guidance and preparation is invaluable, but we can't overlook the vital role you play in your teens' dating relationships.

Mom and Dad, once you've determined that your teen is ready to date, you have to take charge of the "who." You're not powerless in that choice. You can say no when a prospective boyfriend or girlfriend isn't suitable for your teen according to your standards.

Most important is that you have eyes open to the status of a potential boyfriend or girlfriend's walk with the Lord. Ask yourself some questions:

- Is this person my teen wants to date a Christian?
- How long has he/she been walking with the Lord?
- What fruits do I see of that relationship with God?
- What fruits so I see in his/her parents?
- Do I believe they will build each other up in their faith?

When you look at the answers to those questions honestly, I think your answers will become much clearer.

Second only to the decision to follow Christ, marriage is the most important decision your children will make, and it begins with a first date. If dating is approached with few boundaries and plenty of room for compromise, marriage will be too. The concept of a future marriage, as a covenant before God, should be treated with as much nurturing as a person's relationship with God. The boundaries and commitments should be set in stone, and there should be no room for compromise along the way. Then, when believers become yoked together with God, they become like a three-strand cord.

> Though one may be overpowered, two can defend themselves. A cord of **three strands is not quickly broken**. (Eccl. 4:12)

And that, right there, is God's best for marriage.

My good friends Robin Jones Gunn and Tricia Goyer have written an amazing book, *Praying for Your Future Husband*. This book should be required reading for every unmarried girl, and the concept should be shared with every unmarried boy. If they would purpose now—at whatever point they are on their premarriage journey—to pray for that future spouse who is already living, breathing, and making choices, everything would be different. Here's why, in the words of Tricia Goyer and Robin Gunn to "God-lover girls" everywhere:

> When the day comes that your love story is celebrated by your closest friends and family, you'll know that every prayer was worth it. Every whispered word from

a tender heart is precious to God. No request is ignored. No moment spent with your Heavenly Father is wasted.

You might even wish you had prayed more. Why? Because your prayers are the first gifts you will give to your future husband. Gifts in which heaven participates. Gifts sent ahead before the two of you have even met."[2]

Dear God, I need Your help. I see that my duty as a Christian parent requires me to be firm and to protect my kids from poor choices in dating. Please help me always look to You for direction and to see clearly what Your will is. Help me also to gain the respect of my kids so they will follow my guidance without testing the limits. Give them the desire to pursue the path You have laid out before them and to flee from youthful desires and compromise. Thank You for opening my eyes before it's too late. Amen.

CHECK POINTS ▶▶▶

CHECK POINTS

✓ A Christian will never be happy or fulfilled if tethered to someone who constantly pulls in the direction opposite the believer's passionate pursuit of Christ.

✓ Early on in the dating years, set the standard that your teens may only date those who share the same level of faith in God. Prohibit anything less for your kids.

✓ An unequally yoked believer must compromise her faith in order to keep a peaceful home. She can no longer serve God in the way He's called her to—free, open, vibrant—without worrying about how it makes her unbelieving husband feel.

✓ Is God so powerless that He would require you to sacrifice your walk and become unequally yoked in hopes of winning someone to Christ? No way. No human relationship is worth sacrificing your relationship with God.

✓ If every unmarried girl and boy would purpose now—at whatever point they are on their premarriage journey—to pray for that future spouse who is living and breathing, and making choices, everything would be different.

✓ Though one may be overpowered, two can defend themselves. A cord of three strands is not quickly broken (Eccl. 4:12).

Physical Attraction

Is it okay for your tweens and teens to hold hands with their boy-friend or girlfriend? If so, at what age?

How about hugging, or kissing on the cheek?

Oh, you're okay with that? Then what about kissing on the lips? When is it appropriate for young couples to have their first kiss? Do you want to know about it? Would you be shocked if you found out that your twelve-year-old already has?

French kissing—kissing with tongue? Has that come up in any discussions you've had at home?

If you assume it will happen at some point, where should it happen? Certainly not in public, I hope. If in private—well, what are tweens and teens doing with that level of privacy anyway? And how long should the kissing last? A minute? An hour? When does it become too much and how do you plan to regulate this? Or are you too embarrassed to talk about this stuff with your young teens? Maybe you're resting on the fact that it's covered in church and school, and hope you've raised them well enough that they'll make the right choices.

If you are one of those parents who assumes your teen won't go too far, and you're doing nothing to prevent it from happening, then you're reading the right book.

Holding hands ⬎

    Hugging ⬎

        Kissing ⬎

            French kissing ⬎

                Extended making out ⬎

                  Touching over clothes ⬎

                    Groping under clothes ⬎

                          Oral Sex ⬎

                          SEXUAL INTERCOURSE

It's a progression that cannot be undone. If some of that list is okay with you and some of it isn't, then where do you draw the line? What's the definition of *too far* to you, and how are you going to instill that value in your teens without simply laying down a law they haven't ascribed to yet?

Is kissing a sin?

Kissing isn't specifically warned against in the Bible, but lust is. There's no need for Scripture to spell it out in any more detail than this: "Anyone who looks at a woman lustfully has already committed adultery with her in his heart" (Matt. 5:28). This was referring to the act of adultery, but it, like other sins, applies in a broader sense too. We read elsewhere in the Bible that hate equals murder; here we see that lust equals adultery.

For our kids, then, lust is equivalent to premarital sex. Obviously, lust doesn't alter the body the way sexual intercourse does, but it does alter the heart and mind. Passion is meant to be saved for the marriage relationship where it becomes intimacy, not lust.

Have you ever participated in a romantic kiss without feeling stirrings of lust? Sure, it's completely possible to do that. But how do you control when the shift from friendly, casual kissing becomes lustful? If you can't control that shift, how can you expect your teen to manage that? I'm not suggesting that kissing is the same as sex, or that kissing always leads to sin. But it's pretty clear that kissing is a gateway to the next level of physical expression and often does induce lustful stirrings that lead to sin, even if only in the mind.

Passages such as Galatians 5:16–25, Romans 8:1–14, and Colossians 3:5 explain that followers of Christ must avoid succumbing to the temptations and desires of the flesh, since those are not compatible with a sanctified life. Each person, your teens included, have to determine where that line is drawn. Since it's often impossible to see the line until it's crossed, this is where you come in.

> But each person is tempted when they are **dragged away by their own evil desire** and enticed. Then, after desire has conceived, it gives birth to sin; **and sin, when it is full-grown, gives birth to death**. (James 1:14–15)

What comes after kissing?

How do you think your teen would answer the question, what comes after kissing? Maybe with a resounding, "Nothing! That's where it stops for me!"

Wonderful. But what if you pressed it and made him tell you what comes after kissing on the physical ladder? Would he have a grasp on where the physical progression would lead from there? Often, they don't think it through to that level until they're in the situation and feeling the tingly urges. They aren't prepared to turn those desires off. A hand creeps up a shirt, another unbuttons the pants . . . the windows get steamy. Sometimes, in the heat of the moment, someone snaps out of it and calls a halt. But in a family where there's no ongoing dialogue about sexuality, the experience gets filed under, "Hmm . . . interesting."

Next time it goes on for a little longer and a little further. Same thing the next time. Until one day . . . the rest is history.

Should I forbid kissing?

The answer to this question is up to you. Some teens, when carefully guided, choose to wait until marriage to kiss. I do personally know many people who shared their first kisses on their wedding day. How precious and beautiful such a gift would be! And, imagine for a brief moment what their marriages are like and what the divorce rate among those couples is. They have shared something so special with each other and would be loathe to squander that gift by something as weak as divorce.

They made that choice because they saw kissing as more intimate than they wanted to be with anyone but a spouse because they believed it pleased God, and because they wanted to avoid sin. It's completely possible that even kissing would have led them to cross the line to lust, potentially pulling them past the line of purity. After that, their entire lives would have been different.

Others believe that kissing is okay, as long as it ends there. But the flesh is weak, and many cannot stop there. And the trouble is, they won't know they can't stop until it's too late.

What's done can't be undone.

The goal with the hot-buttons discussions you'll be having as you work through this book isn't to hand down a set of rules—though there should definitely be rules—but to achieve in your child a level of commitment borne from a desire to follow God and protect self. So, if a no kissing rule helps keep a teenager from going further, then it's a great commitment.

➤➤➤ **Note:** *There are many issues of sexuality that don't fit neatly under the topic of dating. Today's teens are engaged in all sorts of illicit behavior, regardless of whether they're in dating relationships or not. To prepare yourself for those difficult conversations, see* Hot Buttons Sexuality Edition, *which includes advice for how to raise a virgin, as well as how to have discussions with your kids about what constitutes sex, the truth about teen pregnancy and abortion, and a host of other issues you may not be aware that your teens are already facing.*

Action Steps

With regard to physical attraction and expression, there are some steps you should take:

1. Pray about the physical boundaries you should set in your home.

2. Talk openly with your spouse or other support person about what those boundaries are.

3. Communicate them to your teens and preteens.

4. Set swift and decisive consequences that prove your seriousness.

5. Provide adequate and constant supervision because no matter how well-intentioned your kids are, the heat of the moment is a powerful force.

In the end, Mom and Dad, the choice is yours. This book can equip you to train your kids to think through these issues and hold them up to the light of Scripture. You have the power to take the leadership and raise teens who will respect your guidelines or, at the very least, follow your rules. Dating involves the potential for so much heartache and lifelong devastation—don't leave this vital issue in the hands of an inexperienced teenager to muddle through alone. Help them. Give them proactive strategies that can help prevent future heartache.

It's so scary to be a parent, Lord. I can't imagine doing this without You. Please help me to be a great example of You and a parent worthy of respect. Help my kids to receive my rules and boundaries as they are intended, as a fence around their hearts to keep the wolves from plucking them from my pasture. Now that I'm truly aware of what I need to do, I vow to stay on top of this and open the lines of communication, Lord. I'll do the best I can, but I need Your help in identifying exactly what my boundaries need to be. Help me know when to say yes and when to say no—and how to win my kids over in the process. Please protect them through my efforts. Amen.

CHECK POINTS ➤➤➤

CHECK POINTS

✓ Kissing isn't specifically warned against in the Bible, but lust is.

✓ Obviously, lust doesn't alter the body the way sexual intercourse does, but it does alter the heart and mind. Passion is meant to be saved for the marriage relationship, where it becomes intimacy, not lust.

✓ The goal with the hot-buttons discussions you'll be having as you work through this book isn't to hand down a set of rules—though there should definitely be rules—but to achieve in your child a level of commitment borne from a desire to follow God and protect self.

✓ Dating involves the potential for so much heartache and lifelong devastation—don't leave this vital issue in the hands of an inexperienced teenager to muddle through alone.

✓ "But each person is tempted when they are dragged away by their own evil desire and enticed. Then, after desire has conceived, it gives birth to sin; and sin, when it is full-grown, gives birth to death" (James 1:14–15).

Violence
and Abuse

Several people I spoke to felt the topic of violence was an unnecessary chapter in a book about dating . . . until they saw the statistics.

Let's look at some facts:

> More than 20 percent of all adolescents report having experienced either psychological or physical violence from an intimate partner—and underreporting remains a concern.[3]

As a mom of a fourteen-year-old daughter, this statistic breaks my heart. I look at Natalie and her four best girlfriends and wonder, which one of the five of them is being or has been abused at the hands or words of an adolescent jerk? I can't imagine that any one of them has such low self-esteem as to allow that to happen—but then again, I don't know all of the details of their home lives or their background. The statistics don't lie.

> In a study conducted at a North Carolina university, 66.7 percent of the respondents reported sexual or physical violence with a partner while in high school.[4]

By this statistic, it seems apparent that the older they get, the higher the risk for abuse. By the end of high school, *the minority shifts from those who are abused to those who are not.*

> ➤ In a nationwide survey, 9.8 percent of high school students report being hit, slapped, or physically hurt on purpose by their boyfriend or girlfriend in the twelve months prior to the survey.[5]

Violence seems far removed from the idea of sweet, high school romance. But as the statistics reveal, it's much more common in teen relationships than would even seem possible. While some teens are dealing with crushes and flirtations, others are working to hide bruises and deflect threats—not from the school-yard bully but from their own boyfriends or girlfriends.

Abusers usually want to control their partners over everything from clothing style to food choices. They believe—or at least want their victims to believe—that they are wise and powerful. They often take an approach like *"Wow, you're a mess. It's a good thing I came along. I'll stick around and help you with this mess of a life you have, but you have to trust me implicitly."* Whether or not the abuser verbalizes this, over time, that's what the abused comes to understand and believe.

You are your teens' first line of defense. You have to be on the lookout for any signs of abuse and be willing to end the relationship immediately. But in order to take notice of something that's going on, you have to be around the couple on a regular basis. To achieve this, many families institute a rule that for each date a teenage couple has outside the house, they have to have one in the home or with the parents in some capacity.

I know one mom who makes an "every other" requirement like that, but also adds the caveat that her teens can't date the same person two times in a row without mixing in someone else. This keeps everyone from getting too serious. Smart mama!

Warning Signs

Be alert to and on guard against the possibility of abuse if you have a dating teen. There are always signs; unfortunately, they often go unrecognized until after the fact.

Signs of abuse:
> Bruises and/or unexplained injuries
> Change in appearance
> Dropping friends
> Quitting activities
> Hesitancy to express opinions
> Changes in behavior when boyfriend is around
> Startles easily

Also, many teens shrug off situations where they're being teased in public or called names in private. They need to know that name-calling is a form of abuse and is a precursor to other types of violence. Public disrespect is an unloving behavior and is often a sign that something is wrong.

If you think your teen might be suffering abuse, you should talk to her (or him) about it immediately. Do your best to make the conversation easier by filling in the words and letting your teen simply nod along. Often girls in particular don't come forward with abuse because they believe they deserve it and are afraid to get the abusive partner in trouble. They may also be afraid of being alone since they now feel worthless.

If you find your suspicions were accurate, take immediate action:

> Block the offender's phone number from all cell phones in your home.
> Get into Facebook and other social sites and block any association between the offender and your teen.
> Contact local authorities about a restraining order.
> Press charges if warranted.
> Talk to the abuser's parents and the school administration so everyone is aware.
> Get professional help for your teen so the fallout from this relationship doesn't follow into marriage.

Date Rape

Aside from the ongoing abusive violence we've been discussing so far in this chapter, we also need to look at the issue of date rape. Sometimes this happens by brute physical force, and sometimes it's a drug-facilitated sexual assault.

Sexual assault is any kind of nonconsensual, physical, sexual activity. It can include anything from unwelcome touching to sexual intercourse. Often, date-rapists use powerful drugs—usually slipped into a drink—that make a person dizzy, weak, or confused, unable to defend against or stave off unwanted sexual advances. Sometimes the person has little to no memory of what happened while drugged.

The three most common date-rape drugs are:

◀ *Rohypnol* (roh-HIP-nol). This drug is dissolved in liquid—often a beverage at a bar. Some of its most common names are Circles, Forget Pill, R-2, Rib, Roach, Roofies, Roopies, Rope, and Rophies.
◀ *GHB*, which is short for gamma hydroxybutyric (GAM-muh heye-DROX-

Violence and Abuse

ee-BYOO-tur-ihk) acid. It comes as either a colorless and odorless liquid, a white powder, or a pill. GHB is also known as Bedtime Scoop, G, Gamma 10, Georgia Home Boy, G-Juice, Gook, Goop, Grievous Bodily Harm (GBH), Liquid E, Liquid Ecstasy, Liquid X, and Vita-G.

◀ *Ketamine* (KEET-uh-meen) comes as liquid or a white powder. It's also known as Black Hole, Bump, Cat Valium, Green, Jet, K, K-Hole, Kit Kat, Special K, and Super Acid.

I was the victim of a date-rape situation when I was a young teen. The experience of having my body used without my consent was horrifying. It was probably not drug-induced—though I can't be sure—but it was definitely against my will. I often wonder if I could have stopped what was going on. To be honest, I probably could have. But I was shocked. And feeling guilty. I was somewhere I wasn't supposed to be, and I was drinking alcohol—so I was not clearheaded, and I was worried about getting caught.

Parents, please communicate to your teens that you want them to feel comfortable coming to you about anything, even if they fear getting into trouble. Some parents establish a safe friend their kids can call for a ride, even if they're involved in something very wrong, without fear of punishment. Others have a code they can text or say on a phone call so Mom or Dad will know they need help.

Action Steps

The prevalence of abuse among dating teens is a huge reason why it's so important for you to be involved in every aspect of your teens' relationships. You should:

- Limit the amount of time spent with a date.
- Limit the frequency of outings or time spent together.
- Prepare your teen for the warning signs of abuse.
- Clearly outline what types of behavior are not okay.
- Provide your teens with a safety net—a way they can feel safe in reaching out to you for help.
- Spend time with your teens and anyone who might become a regular date/boyfriend/girlfriend.
- Be prepared to say no to any potential relationship.
- Bathe it in prayer.
- Go with your gut.

Prayerfully, if you prepare your teens well, you'll never need to call upon the information in this chapter and the other resources out there for victims of rape and violence.

Oh, Lord, how it must grieve Your heart to see Your precious children abused, degraded, and belittled. I struggle to believe that my teens would let this happen to them, so please open my eyes and make me aware, so I can help them when I need to. Please protect them from evil and guide them on Your path of righteousness. Let them see themselves the way You do and never fall for the jabs of the enemy who wants them to believe they're worthless. Let me be an extension of Your love for them. Amen.

CHECK POINTS

✓ More than 20 percent of all adolescents report having experienced either psychological or physical violence.

✓ While some teens are dealing with crushes and flirtations, others are working to hide bruises and deflect threats—not from the school-yard bully but from their own boyfriends or girlfriends.

✓ By the end of high school, the minority shifts from those who are abused to those who are not.

✓ You are your teens' first line of defense.

✓ Name-calling is a form of abuse and is a precursor to other types of violence.

✓ Public disrespect is an unloving behavior and is often a sign that something is wrong.

✓ Often girls in particular don't come forward with abuse because they believe they deserve it and are afraid to get the abusive partner in trouble. They may also be afraid of being alone since they now feel worthless.

PART THREE

Pressing the Dating HOT BUTTONS

We've discussed the hows, whys, and whens of dating. We've looked at Scripture. We've addressed the probabilities of what your teens will face in the coming days, or what they've already encountered in relationships with the opposite sex. Now it's your turn. It's time to take a stand in your home and claim your teens' hearts and minds for the Lord.

It takes work to reach the hearts of teenagers and help them become conscientious servants of God who take ownership of their own choices and responsibility for all that passes in front of their eyes. It takes hard work to lead your teens to choose God's ways over the world's ways and to deny themselves the immediate gratification that comes with sin and wrong or premature choices.

Are you ready?

Protective Procedures

The first few chapters of this book identified why it's necessary to press the hot buttons with your kids about issues that affect their lives in big ways. Part 2 outlined specific aspects of dating that you need to be attentive to. Now we're going to actually implement strategies to affect real change and a lasting impact. I won't lie; it's going to take lots of work—and some of it will be uncomfortable. Are you ready for that? Are you convinced that you must put the time in with your teen and wage the battles to win the war?

First, let's summarize what you can do, Mom and Dad, to prepare the hearts and minds of your teens to make good dating decisions.

Respect in General

◀ When it comes to being a parent your teens will respect, the most important thing you can do is spend time with them.

- Be available and approachable at any time, for any reason. It doesn't matter if you get awakened three hours after you've fallen asleep and it concerns something you don't see as an emergency—treat it as the most important thing on the planet. How you handle those situations will determine whether your kids come to you with the big stuff and trust that you'll respond as a parent to their immediate needs, fears, and concerns.

- Go ahead and make mistakes. You're not perfect, and your teens don't want you to pretend you are. When you're real about your own shortcomings, they feel safer in admitting theirs. Don't be afraid to say, "I'm sorry."

- Guard against criticism and focus on encouragement. People erect walls when they feel criticized, and generally shut out even the constructive points.

- Set the bar high for your teens, but keep your standards realistic and achievable. To get the results you seek, you need to be a loving guide—not a brutal authoritarian.

When It Comes to Dating

- Make your home a place your teens and their friends want to hang out. Keep your teens close . . . and their dates closer!

- Start early. Help them anticipate dating the right person at the right time. Teach them the truth about romances they see on TV and in movies. Share with your teens the complexities of dating relationships and ways to keep appropriate boundaries with members of the opposite sex.

- Help your teens establish realistic expectations about male-female relationships. Try to limit or eliminate fantasy outlooks on the future. If they're looking for magic, they're going to search and search until they discover it isn't real.

- Set an example of respectful relationships. Have intelligent and respectful conversations in their presence. Show affection to your spouse and receive it graciously. Don't argue, but go ahead and disagree without anger.

- Read *Hot Buttons Sexuality Edition* and talk to your teens about their sexuality.

- Share clear boundaries and consequences, and then be prepared to follow through. The very first time you don't follow through, you send a message of weakness and lack of commitment.

When it comes to dating (and anything really), you get to pick the whats, whens, wheres, hows, and whos. Decide ahead of time what you're going to allow, and express it clearly, with no room for debate. Some things you need to decide now:

- **Curfews.** These can be different for each child, different for the age range, or even adjusted per event. It's completely up to you how you handle this. But you must set firm consequences and be prepared to stick to them should curfew be broken.

- **Quantity.** Double dates only, or are single dates okay? Single dates only with certain people or to certain places? Who decides?

- **Age differences.** You can set a requirement about the age range of boyfriends or girlfriends if that's something you're concerned about.

- **Rules about changes.** When do your teens need to let you know if plans have changed?

- **Reachability.** Always within a phone call—never out of reach. The phone must be answered or the call returned within ten minutes— or some kind of rule that you deem appropriate. With my kids, the privilege of carrying a cell phone requires them to be accessible to me first and foremost. If not, they must not need the phone. (Works every time.)

- **Physical boundaries.** Discuss this as a family so your teens can take ownership in the decision. Then, Mom and Dad, you decide what is allowed physically, and set accountability checkpoints.

- **Rotation dates.** A great way to limit the possibility of getting too serious with one person is to require that your teens go out on a date with someone else before they can date the prior person again.

- **Rotating places.** One date out on the town, the next one at home with Mom and Dad nearby.

- **Consequences.** No matter which rule or boundary we're talking about, you need to set the consequences in stone and be prepared to follow through.

While the world laughs as we continue to abide by biblical standards, Christian parents must be prepared to stand in the gap for their children, even in terms of dating. Sometimes we will need to make unpopular decisions, but I believe they will pay off in the long run.

As previously mentioned, Christian parents need to be available to their children. We must discuss issues such as dating and what behavior is acceptable for Christian young people. As parents, we must have our proverbial doors open at all times so our children are comfortable coming to us with questions about life and love. Teens should not have to answer these questions alone. Allowing them to decide for themselves, or worse, making their decisions based on what they see on television, is setting them up for failure.

As parents, we must constantly recall Ephesians 6:4: "Fathers, do not irritate and provoke your children to anger [do not exasperate them to resentment], but rear them [tenderly] in the training and discipline and the counsel and admonition of the Lord" (AMP). If we live out this verse, our children will have the values of Christ instilled within them and we can prayerfully trust that they will one day be ready to thrive as Christians amid the challenges of dating.

>>> Challenge: *Pray with your teens before they walk out of the house for a date. Sounds easy enough? Well, I don't mean to pray only with your teenager before the date arrives. I mean, pray with and for them both, no matter what, before they're allowed to go on the date—any date.*

Prayer might be the one thing that changes everything for your dating teens. Praying with them right before they leave the house not only sets the tone for the evening, but it invites God into their midst. It focuses them on Him and lets them know that you aren't kidding. If you decide to allow dating, and your teen is at that threshold, take this final step toward ensuring the best possible outcome.

This prayer is easy, Lord. Help me. Show me what I need to do, and help me do it. Please. Amen.

CHECK POINTS >>>

CHECK POINTS

✓ Guard against criticism and focus on encouragement. People erect walls when they feel criticized, and generally shut out even the constructive points.

✓ Make your home a place your teens and their friends want to hang out. Keep your teens close . . . and their dates closer!

✓ Parents, you get to pick the whats, whens, wheres, hows, and whos. Decide ahead of time what you're going to allow and express it clearly, with no room for debate.

✓ No matter which rule or boundary we're talking about, you need to set the consequences in stone and be prepared to follow through.

✓ As parents, we must have our proverbial doors open at all times so our children are comfortable coming to us with questions about life and love.

✓ Pray with your teens before they walk out of the house for a date.

The Armor
of God

As it pertains to the hot-button issues of dating, the "armor of God" is not simply a word picture in Scripture but a practical resource for navigating the spiritual battles Christ-followers face. Before you move forward to attack these dating hot buttons in the next few chapters, I want to lead you through a symbolic application of the armor of God.

Below, you'll find a breakdown of Ephesians 6:10–17. Each phrase is followed by a bit of commentary and application, and a few directions. But please take note, there is nothing divinely prescribed in these specific directions. Perhaps there are other actions you can take that will hold greater meaning for you; in that case, feel free to improvise. However, please take this seriously. More than a silly exercise, this is a physical display of your faith in God's power and your acceptance of His protections.

Be strong in the Lord and in his mighty power. (Eph. 6:10)

Mom and Dad, you're not alone. All of the strength and wisdom you need to be a godly parent is yours. You don't have to have all of the answers about dating and purity—He does. You don't have to see the future—He does. You don't have to make up for the past—He did.

Do this: Raise your open hands in surrender, ready to receive from God and expectant that He'll grant you strength, wisdom, and grace.

Pray this: *Lord, please help me stand strong in the power of Your might. Help me to let go of my need to control and to fully surrender my family to You. Let me rest in Your power and walk as a parent in Your strength. Guide my senses with Your knowledge and help me to know what I need to know, when I need to know it.*

Put on the full armor of God, so that you can take your stand against the devil's schemes. (Eph. 6:11)

God has already provided your protection and has already secured your ultimate victory in this battle—even if the battle seems daunting at times. Remember the promise in Philippians 1:6, where it says that He started the work [in your teens], and He'll finish it. He stands ready to uphold you as you face the enemy who seeks to pull your teens down a slippery slope.

The Armor of God

Do this: Gird your shoulders; plant your feet. Stand proud like a soldier waiting for orders.

Pray this: *Prepare my body to receive Your armor. Place it carefully that I might be protected as a parent. Then, protect my teens in the same way, Father—their eyes, hands, mouths, and bodies—and guard their desires and decisions. Let them run from danger and stand strong against temptation.*

> For **our struggle is not against flesh and blood**, but against the rulers, against the authorities, against the powers of this dark world and **against the spiritual forces of evil** in the heavenly realms. (Eph. 6:12)

You see, your real fight isn't against the boyfriends or girlfriends. It isn't against the desires that lurk inside every human being. And it isn't against your teen. It's against the enemy who seeks to destroy and often uses physical temptation in dating relationships to achieve that.

Do this: Place your hands on your teen's bedroom door.

Pray this: *Father, I surrender this child, whom You love with a passion far greater than even I, to You. I call on Your mighty power to fight against our enemy who has no place in this family. We choose this day whom we will serve; we choose to serve You. And I claim Your promises over the inhabitants of this home.*

Therefore put on **the full armor of God**, so that **when the day of evil comes**, you may be able to **stand your ground**, and after you have done everything, to stand. (Eph. 6:13)

Armor is the barricade between the enemy's attempts to cripple the followers of God and your heart, mind, and body. With the armor of God in place, he is ultimately powerless against you. We've read the end of the Book—we win! But though that ultimate victory is assured, we may feel like we lose some of the battles along the way. That's when we need to rest in God's power and rely on His promises. It's all a process and we need not worry about the individual battles if our eyes are set on victory over the war.

Do this: Close your eyes and imagine impenetrable steel covering every inch of your teen's body.

Pray this: *With armor in place, make my child an indestructible force to bring glory to Your kingdom as we stand together against the enemy.*

Stand firm then, with **the belt of truth** buckled around your waist . . . (Eph. 6:14a)

During times of battle, the tunic was belted to secure the soldier's clothes and keep every part of the armor in place, allowing him to move more freely.

The Armor of God

Do this: Buckle a proverbial belt around your waist. Then imagine that your kids are standing in front of you, and go through the motions of putting a belt on each of them.

Pray this: *With Your truth around our waists, let it restrain our fleshly desires and poor choices and lead us on Your path.*

. . . with the **breastplate of righteousness** in place . . . (Eph. 6:14b)

The breastplate protects the heart.

Do this: Symbolically, don the breastplate; then place it upon your kids.

Pray this: *Let Your righteousness, oh Lord, be a shield about this family. Our protector and the lifter of our heads.*

. . . and with your feet **fitted with the readiness** that comes from **the gospel of peace**. (Eph. 6:15)

You're ready. You have the information you need and you're covered in prayer. In the next chapters, you're going to actually implement the principles of getting and staying battle ready.

Do this: Lift each foot and plant it down hard.

Pray this: *I am confident in Your Word, Lord. I believe that You have led me and prepared me to be my teens' wisest counsel and guide. Help me exhibit patience and strength.*

> In addition to all this, take up **the shield of faith**, with which you can extinguish all the flaming arrows of the evil one. (Eph. 6:16)

Notice, the shield is active, not simply defensive. You're not blocking the enemy's arrows and sending them back out to do damage somewhere else; you're extinguishing them. Apply that truth to the temptations and desires that lurk in the world of dating.

Do this: Raise your arm as though you hold a shield and wave it in front of you. Imagine your kids standing before you, and wave it in front of them also.

Pray this: *Put out the flames of peer pressure and temptation, Lord. Let this shield of my faith swallow them whole that they would disappear.*

Take the **helmet of salvation** . . . (Eph. 6:17a)

The helmet protects the mind from doubt, fear, anger, carelessness, and apathy.

Do this: Place the helmet of salvation securely over your head, to your shoulders. Reach out in front of you and do the same as though your teens stood before you.

Pray this: *I rest in my salvation, Lord. You are mighty to save and faithful to preserve.*

. . . and the **sword of the Spirit**, which is the word of God. (Eph. 6:17b)

You're armed and ready to fight. In the following chapters, I will walk you through the next action steps in your battle for your teens.

Do this: Raise your sword, which is the Bible—the Word of God.

Pray this: *I am equipped and ready to fight Satan's schemes against my teens. I need You to guide me and show me what my next move should be. Keep my heart and mind open to the truths and possibilities of what my kids face. And help them, Lord, to have the strength to say no, the wisdom to walk away, and the passion to chase hard after You. Amen.*

Strategic Scenarios

Here's where the fun really begins! Using Strategic Scenarios, you'll be putting your tween(s) and/or teen(s) into pressure-filled situations by telling some short stories. You'll then present a few optional responses to the dilemma from which they will choose the most natural personal responses. From there, you'll be guided to lead them through several discussion points, and referred back to material given previously in this book. It's very important that you have these discussions with absolutely no judgment about the choices they make.

Even though some of the scenarios are written specifically with a particular gender in mind, you should still guide your teens through them and help them see the viewpoint from the other side. Many times they will learn more from the opposite perspective, so don't skip over scenarios that don't seem to apply.

The important thing, when you begin this process, is to pray for guidance. You want to be open to the leading of the Holy Spirit so you can discern when to push an issue, and when to let it be.

You don't have to pretend you're making all this up as some big stroke of genius. It's okay to admit you're reading a book and this practice was suggested. After all, why not show your kids that you vigorously pursue new ways to reach and teach them? Trust me, once you begin, even if you're simply reading from the book at first, the conversation will develop; kids are desperate to work this stuff out.

In my family, these worked best around the dinner table. Sometimes we'd get through two or three over the course of a meal, but often just one would spark enough discussion and we wouldn't get any further. That's okay—in fact, that's wonderful. Communication is the goal, so don't stifle that in order to move on to the next scenario.

Some other places you might open Strategic Scenarios discussions are:

- in the car
- in a waiting room
- on a walk or bike ride
- while on a family date night

So, pretty much anywhere a conversation can take place!

If you have children of varying ages, don't shy away from doing these together. I'm a firm believer in getting the issues out on the table well in advance of the peer pressure. So, if your slightly younger children are going to be introduced to a concept relatively soon anyway, you'd much rather it come a bit sooner through these controlled and monitored means.

As you approach each topic, be careful not to preach. Allow your kids the freedom to work out the issue in this safe environment. Enjoy this process as it opens the lines of communication in your family.

Parents, tell your teen this story.

You've liked this one boy for a really long time. He finally asks you out on a date. The only problem is that you're not allowed to date for another year. If you say no, he'll probably ask someone else and then you'll have missed your one shot at the boy of your dreams. What do you do?

Now offer the following options with no personal commentary.

Let your teen think about the choices and make an honest decision.

> **A.** You thank him for the offer, but tell him you're not allowed. You let him know you hope he'll still be interested in a year.
>
> **B.** Beg your parents to let you go. Cry if you have to.
>
> **C.** You go out with him anyway, and tell your parents you're going out with friends.
>
> **D.** Plan an outing with friends—both guys and girls—so you can be together without it being perceived as a "date."

Crucial Step

Use this scenario to guide a discussion about early dating choices. Be very careful not to sound judgmental or accusatory. Remember, your teen is exploring thoughts and first impressions—these aren't actual choices . . . yet. Parents, from this scenario, you can see how vital it is to start these conversations and set up your boundaries early, *before* your teens are allowed to date, so there's no mistaking the expectations.

Discussion Points

- Why did you make the choice you did?
- No boy who cares about you will want you to lie.
- There's no rush.
- If he isn't interested in waiting, then he wasn't going to stick around for a long time anyway.
- How do you feel about our dating restrictions?
- Do you understand why the rules are what they are?
- Would it be respectful to beg for them to be altered in a circumstance like this?
- Do you have a different view on this scenario than you did at the start? Why or why not?
- Would you like to change your answer or stick with it?

Children, **obey your parents** in everything, for this **pleases the Lord**.

(Col. 3:20)

Parents, tell your teen this story.

You're out with friends at the mall. A boy you've liked for a long time joins the group. Suddenly, your friends decide they have to leave, and you realize you've been "set up" on a date. Now you have to decide if you should call home and tell your parents what happened. He's really cute, and you want to stay with him, but know you'd get in huge trouble if you did. What do you do?

Now offer the following options with no personal commentary.

Let your teen think about the choices and make an honest decision.

> A. You call home right away. It wasn't your fault your friends did that, but lying and sneaking around would be.
>
> B. He agrees to disappear when it's time for your dad to show up, so you stay and hang out with him.
>
> C. You stay for a while, and then break away to call home. This way, Cute Boy doesn't need to find out you can't date, and Mom and Dad don't need to know exactly how long you stayed there alone with a boy.
>
> D. You text your friends and demand they come back, so you won't get in trouble for being alone with him, but can still hang out.

Crucial Step

Use this scenario to guide a discussion about dating choices and trust. Be very careful not to sound judgmental or accusatory. Remember, your teen is exploring thoughts and first impressions—these aren't actual choices . . . yet. Mom and Dad, now's not the time to establish or rehash rules. Allow the discussion to take its course. Set aside a separate time for clearly establishing what the rules are and how you expect your teens to respond.

Discussion Points

- Why did you make the choice you did?
- It's a quick step over the line from innocent to guilty.
- No relationship should start with dishonesty.
- The hard thing is often the right thing.
- How would you feel about friends who did that, knowing you weren't allowed to date?
- Are there levels of honesty, or is a lie a lie?
- Do you have a different view on this scenario than you did at the start? Why or why not?
- Would you like to change your answer or stick with it?

If anyone, then, **knows the good they ought to do** and doesn't do it, it is sin for them.
(James 4:17)

Parents, tell your teen this story.

You've liked this girl for ages. Now that you're finally allowed to date, you're looking forward to asking her out. The problem is, your best friend is going out with her. He doesn't even like her all that much, and he knew you liked her. So, really, he's the one in the wrong because he shouldn't have gone after her, knowing you wanted to. But now he won't back off. What do you do?

Now offer the following options with no personal commentary.

Let your teen think about the choices and make an honest decision.

> **A.** He's totally wrong, and you're not going to let someone else's power struggle keep you from this girl. He can get over it—or not. His choice.
>
> **B.** You refuse to choose between your friend and this girl. He can have her for now, but you're pretty sure he'll dump her soon. You can go after her then.
>
> **C.** No girl is worth losing a friendship. You pick your friend, give up on the girl for now, and hope he doesn't act like this again.
>
> **D.** You choose neither. No girl is worth losing a friend, but no real friend would have acted like he did.

Crucial Step

Use this scenario to guide a discussion about dating and friendship choices. Be very careful not to sound judgmental or accusatory. Remember, your teen is exploring thoughts and first impressions—these aren't actual choices . . . yet. Mom and Dad, where friendship and dating are concerned, teens are interested in hearing about your own experience—good and bad—just be sure it doesn't monopolize the conversation. One relevant story is enough for one conversation.

Discussion Points

- Why did you make the choice you did?
- What's more important? A friendship or a dating relationship?
- Who was more wrong in this scenario: you or your friend?
- What about the girl? Did she have any say in the matter?
- Should a friend make another friend choose like that?
- Do you have a different view on this scenario than you did at the start? Why or why not?
- Would you like to change your answer or stick with it?

Wounds from **a friend** can be **trusted**, but an enemy multiplies kisses.
(Prov. 27:6)

Parents, tell your teen this story.

All of your friends are dating, but you don't really want to deal with the intense drama and heartbreak you see happening to them. You're even considering waiting until after high school to date at all. But you know that if you decide you don't want to have a relationship at this point in your life, your friends will think you're weird. What do you do?

Now offer the following options with no personal commentary.

Let your teen think about the choices and make an honest decision.

> A. Stay true to your instincts and wait until you're older, deciding that true friends will be proud of you and may even secretly admire you for your stand.
>
> B. You decide to go on a date with someone who agrees ahead of time to just be friends, so your friends won't think you're weird.
>
> C. Why fight it? You don't feel quite right about it, but that's better than getting teased or having people wonder if you're gay.
>
> D. *Are you kidding?* Not dating is so not an option for you!

Crucial Step

Use this scenario to guide a discussion about dating choices and peer pressure. Be very careful not to sound judgmental or accusatory. Remember, your teen is exploring thoughts and first impressions—these aren't actual choices . . . yet. Parents, remember how strong peer pressure was in your own life, and be slow to judge that in your kids' lives. Instead, ground them in God's Word so they're more confident in going against the flow.

Discussion Points
- Why did you make the choice you did?
- Why do you feel that you need to do something just because your friends are?
- Not dating until your late teens, or later, is a great choice.
- What can I do as your parent to help you stick to your commitments?
- How could you answer your friends' questions and explain this to them?
- If you feel the need to date, why is that?
- Discuss chapter 5.
- Do you have a different view on this scenario than you did at the start? Why or why not?
- Would you like to change your answer or stick with it?

But if **we hope** for what we do not yet have, **we wait for it patiently**.

(Rom. 8:25)

Parents, tell your teen this story.

Your friend's parents don't allow her to date yet. She wants you to cover for her so she can go out with a boy she likes. She'll sleep over at your house after the date, so it's not a complete lie. What do you do?

Now offer the following options with no personal commentary.

Let your teen think about the choices and make an honest decision.

> A. Sure, why not? It's not like you're breaking any of the rules at your house. The rules your friend breaks are her own business.
>
> B. You don't quite feel comfortable with the situation, so you come up with a compromise. She can spend the night, and you invite the boy to your house to hang out while she's there.
>
> C. You tell her no. You don't want to participate in a lie.
>
> D. You encourage her to come clean with her parents.

Crucial Step

Use this scenario to guide a discussion about dating choices and lying. Be very careful not to sound judgmental or accusatory. Remember, your teen is exploring thoughts and first impressions—these aren't actual choices . . . yet. Mom and Dad, this scenario is a great reminder to get the whole story when your kids plan activities with their friends.

Discussion Points

- Why did you make the choice you did?
- What is a lie?
- What if something happened while she was out with him?
- Is your reputation with other adults important to you?
- What about talking to your friend about waiting?
- No boy is worth sneaking around to see. The right kind of boy wouldn't even want you to.
- Do you have a different view on this scenario than you did at the start? Why or why not?
- Would you like to change your answer or stick with it?

The LORD detests lying lips, but **he delights** in people **who are trustworthy**.

(Prov. 12:22)

Parents, tell your teen this story.

You're hanging out at your boyfriend's house and his parents aren't home—which is against the rules. You're looking through the books on the bookshelf and he comes up behind you, puts his hands on your shoulders and gently turns you around. You know what's coming—he's going to kiss you. You like him a lot, but you're not ready for a first kiss with him or anyone. What do you do?

Now offer the following options with no personal commentary.

Let your teen think about the choices and make an honest decision.

> A. You reach up and take his hands from your shoulders and tell him you're not ready for that.
>
> B. You don't want to be completely honest, so you turn your face and let him kiss your cheek. Then you tell him you have a cold.
>
> C. You're horrified that he doesn't know you well enough or doesn't care about you enough to know you're not ready. You ask him to take you home. He's not the kind of boy you want to date.
>
> D. You go ahead and kiss him. Everyone needs a first kiss; might as well get it over with.

Crucial Step

Use this scenario to guide a discussion about dating and physical activity. Be very careful not to sound judgmental or accusatory. Remember, your teen is exploring thoughts and first impressions—these aren't actual choices . . . yet. Mom and Dad, be sure you have a plan in place, should your teen find themselves unexpectedly in a compromising situation. Who can they call? What should they do if you're unavailable?

Discussion Points

* Why did you make the choice you did?
* Your convictions are worth more than giving in just to make a boy happy.
* A few seconds can change a lot. You can't get back your first kiss.
* Chapter 6 has a lot of information about kissing and physical activity.
* Do you have a different view on this scenario than you did at the start? Why or why not?
* Would you like to change your answer or stick with it?

Finally brothers and sisters, whatever is **true**, whatever is **noble**, whatever is **right**, whatever is **pure**, whatever is **lovely**, whatever is **admirable**— if anything is excellent or praiseworthy—**think about such things**. Whatever you have learned or received or heard from me, or seen in me—put it into practice. And the God of peace will be with you.

(Phil. 4:8–9)

Parents, tell your teen this story.

You've been going out with someone for about eight months. You get along really well, and you generally have a good relationship. The only thing is, she kind of makes fun of you in front of other people. She isn't viciously mean, just little jabs and digs now and then. And, when you're alone and arguing, she sometimes resorts to name-calling. What should you do about it?

Now offer the following options with no personal commentary.

Let your teen think about the choices and make an honest decision.

> **A.** If that's as far as it goes and you really like this person, you'll stay but have a talk with her later.
>
> **B.** You start trading jabs and putting her down as much as she puts you down. If she doesn't like it, she can leave.
>
> **C.** You talk to a youth pastor or school counselor for advice—maybe you can go together.
>
> **D.** You're out of there. There's no way to get past the hurt caused when she said that stuff to you.

Crucial Step

Use this scenario to begin a discussion about dating and self-respect. Be very careful not to sound judgmental or accusatory. Remember, your teen is exploring thoughts and first impressions—these aren't actual choices . . . yet. Parents, remember that whatever your kids experience at home, that is what they consider "normal." If you demean your spouse or kids, or allow yourself to be demeaned, they will take their cues from you and come to expect that in relationships.

Discussion Points
- Why did you make the choice you did?
- Review chapter 8 about dating violence.
- Public disrespect is an unloving behavior and is often a sign that something is wrong.
- Name-calling is a form of abuse and is a precursor to other types of violence.
- The next step is physical.
- How would you feel if you saw your friend or sibling being treated that way?
- Would you feel loved in that relationship?
- What might motivate an abused person to stay in a bad relationship?
- Pray that God will protect you from ever being in a situation like this.
- What are the steps you'd take to get out of this situation?
- Do you have a different view on this scenario than you did at the start? Why or why not?
- Would you like to change your answer or stick with it?

Out of respect **for Christ**, be courteously **reverent to one another**. (Eph. 5:21 MSG)

Parents, tell your teen this story.

You're dating someone, but you really like her BFF more—she's much cuter and more popular. You've even been secretly hanging out together, and it's clear you have more in common. It really does seem to be a better fit, and even she thinks so. The problem is, your girlfriend would be crushed if you broke up with her—and totally devastated if you got together with her best friend. What do you do?

Now offer the following options with no personal commentary.

Let your teen think about the choices and make an honest decision.

> A. Life's too short to worry about all of those details. You follow your heart, and make things happen with the girl you really want.
>
> B. Just start acting distant with your girlfriend. When she realizes that things aren't going well, she'll probably break up with you, and then you'll be free to date whomever you want.
>
> C. You realize you're not happy in your current relationship, so that has to end. Even though you want to get together with the other girl right away, you decide to give it a few weeks so it's not so painful for your ex.
>
> D. It's obviously time to move on from the current relationship, but no way are you going to get together with the other girl. She's shown her true colors by trying to hook up with her best friend's boyfriend. That's not the kind of girl you want to date—no matter how hot she is.

Crucial Step

Use this scenario to begin a discussion about dating and loyalty. Be very careful not to sound judgmental or accusatory. Remember, your teen is exploring thoughts and first impressions—these aren't actual choices . . . yet. Encourage your teen to consider this scenario from the perspective of each of the participants.

Discussion Points

- Why did you make the choice you did?
- What qualities do you look for in a girlfriend?
- What do you think about the backstabbing friend?
- Does hotness override loyalty when you rank important qualities?
- What are some signs that a relationship should end?
- What's your responsibility in ending a relationship? How should it be done?
- Do you think a person's actions should reflect on their friends and boyfriend or girlfriend?
- Do you have a different view on this scenario than you did at the start? Why or why not?
- Would you like to change your answer or stick with it?

Charm is deceptive, and beauty is fleeting; but **a woman who fears the Lord** is to be praised. Honor her for all that her hands have done, and let **her works bring her praise** at the city gate.

(Prov. 31:30–31)

Parents, tell your teen this story.

You got in a big argument with your boyfriend last night because he was flirting with another girl right in front of you. He said it was your fault because you weren't paying any attention to him. Then he got really mad and pushed you into a chair. When the chair broke, you hit your head on the wall and have a bump above your eye. You're sure he didn't mean to do it, and he's been texting and apologizing all day long. It's kind of sweet the way he's gushing over you to get you to forgive him, and now he wants to take you out to make up for it. What do you do?

Now offer the following options with no personal commentary.

Let your teen think about the choices and make an honest decision.

A. It was only the first time something like that happened, so it's your duty to forgive him and move on. Now you have to decide what to wear for your special date tonight! Makeup should cover the bruise.

B. You can forgive him, but you're not quite ready to be alone with him. You invite him to just hang out at your house, hoping your parents don't notice the bruise.

C. There is no way you're going out with him again—ever! But you have no plans to tell anyone what happened either. It's too embarrassing that you basically got beat up by your boyfriend. That stuff only happens in movies!

D. He's history! And not only are you going to tell your parents, but you're taking pictures of the bump and the broken chair in case the police want them.

Crucial Step

Use this scenario to guide a discussion about abuse and violence in dating relationships. Be very careful not to sound judgmental or accusatory. Remember, your teen is exploring thoughts and first impressions—these aren't actual choices . . . yet. Parents, here is your chance to affirm to your kids that their physical, emotional, and spiritual safety is of utmost importance to you. And if physical boundaries are often violated in your own home, if "accidents" happen, it is time to seek the advice of a pastor or counselor.

Discussion Points

- Why did you make the choice you did?
- What is abuse?
- What is the likelihood an abusive person will change completely?
- Are there ways you can help this person without putting yourself at risk?
- What are the legal ramifications of violence like this?
- If you stayed together, what would the future look like?
- What are accountability partners?
- Maybe it's time for some alone time with God to heal from this situation.
- Chapter 8 covers this topic in detail.
- When do you share hints of violence or temper outbursts with your parents?
- The National Domestic Violence hotline can be found at www.thehotline. org and at 1-877-799-SAFE (7233), or 1-800-787-3224 (TTY).
- Do you have a different view on this scenario than you did at the start? Why or why not?
- Would you like to change your answer or stick with it?

Drive out the mocker, and out goes strife; quarrels and **insults are ended**.
(Prov. 22:10)

Strategic Scenario 10

Parents, tell your teen this story.

You're eighteen, and you've dated several guys, but none of those relationships have lasted longer than a few weeks. You're waiting for someone special to have a long-term relationship with. Finally! The guy you've had your eye on for a long time asks you out. You're so excited—this could be it . . . He could be the one!

Your date goes really well. You know you look great together, you have a lot in common, and you're both Christians. What could go wrong? Then, in the car after dinner, he leans over to kiss you. After a few minutes, he starts groping around and puts his hand under your shirt while his kisses move to your neck. What do you do?

Now offer the following options with no personal commentary.

Let your teen think about the choices and make an honest decision.

> A. You're ready for whatever. This guy is too good to lose because you're chicken. At eighteen, you should have been doing some of this stuff anyway. Everyone else does.
>
> B. You laugh and tell him to stop. You can't really blame him for trying, but you hope he'll respect your boundaries—at least for now.
>
> C. You're shocked that he would try that on the first date—or any date—since he's supposed to be a Christian like you. You ask him to take you home; he just wasn't the person you thought he was.
>
> D. You get out of the car and call your parents to come pick you up.

Crucial Step

Use this scenario to guide a discussion about physical boundaries. Be very careful not to sound judgmental or accusatory. Your teen is exploring thoughts and first impressions—these aren't actual choices . . . yet. Parents, remember, you're guiding your kids to make righteous and healthy choices for themselves, not just training them to follow rules. The latter may help make your parenting job easier, but the former will influence them into adulthood and have a positive impact on their lives.

Discussion Points

- Why did you make the choice you did?
- What would happen in this relationship if you went with it?
- What are your boundaries?
- Where would the groping and kissing stop?
- Can you be sure you could enforce your boundaries in the heat of the moment?
- What is the mark of a Christian?
- Do his actions mean this boy isn't a Christian?
- Read chapter 7 about physical activity and dating.
- Read *Hot Buttons Sexuality Edition* to delve deeper into this subject.
- Would you talk to your mom or dad about this situation? Why or why not?
- Do you have a different view on this scenario than you did at the start? Why or why not?
- Would you like to change your answer or stick with it?

Don't let anyone look down on you because you are young, but **set an example** for the believers in speech, in conduct, in love, **in faith and in purity**.

(1 Tim. 4:12)

Parents, tell your teen this story.

You're out with a guy for the first time, and it happens to be a school dance. You don't know him very well since he just moved to town. He seems to really like you because he keeps looking at you, and then looks away when you catch his eye. It's cute how he's so nervous! You notice him say something to his friend, then order at the concession stand. A few minutes later, he's walking toward you with two drinks in his hand and holds one out to you. Mom and Dad have always said not to accept a drink from anyone if you didn't see it being poured, and then to keep your eyes on it the entire time. Plus, it took a long time for him to bring it to you. But you sure don't want to hurt his feelings. What do you do?

Now offer the following options with no personal commentary.

Let your teen think about the choices and make an honest decision.

A. You're parched and, besides, you're at a school dance—what could he have done, really? You eagerly accept the drink and thank him.

B. You thank him and set the drink down. When he's not looking, you'll sniff and take a small sip to be sure it's just Coke. If anything's weird, you'll knock it over and pretend it spilled.

C. You smile, say no thanks to the drink, and ask if he wants to dance. You would never drink something you hadn't ordered or poured yourself.

D. He seems friendly and harmless and you've never gotten a bad feeling about him, but you reach for the drink in his other hand, just to be safe.

Crucial Step

Use this scenario to guide a discussion about physical safety and accepting drinks from strangers. Be very careful not to sound judgmental or accusatory. Remember, your teen is exploring thoughts and first impressions—these aren't actual choices . . . yet. Parents, whether you allow your kids to go to a dance is not the issue. Make sure to keep the focus of this scenario on your teen's safety in unknown situations.

Discussion Points

- Why did you make the choice you did?
- What could happen if you accepted the drink?
- Read chapter 8.
- What's the rule about this?
- What if you bought the drink yourself, but then went to the restroom and left your drink unattended for a few minutes?
- Do you have a different view on this scenario than you did at the start? Why or why not?
- Would you like to change your answer or stick with it?

Trust in the LORD with all your heart and lean **not on your own understanding**.

(Prov. 3:5)

Parents, tell your teen this story.

You've been seeing this girl for a while and you really like her. She's everything you thought you wanted in a girlfriend, and she really seems into you too. Last night, while you were kissing in the car, she whispered, "I love you." You didn't say anything back to her because you don't want to throw those words around lightly, but you don't want to lose her either. Maybe you do love her . . . but you just don't know. What do you do?

Now offer the following options with no personal commentary.

Let your teen think about the choices and make an honest decision.

> A. They're just words. It's much better to tell someone you love her than to be hurtful and not say it. Besides, you don't want to lose this girl. You plan to tell her first next time.
>
> B. You have an honest talk with her and let her know that it's nothing against her but you're saving those words for now.
>
> C. You decide that if it happens again, you'll just say, "Thanks, that means a lot to me." If she gets upset because you won't say it back, that's for her to deal with.
>
> D. You plan to say it because if you tell her you love her, maybe she'll have sex with you.

Crucial Step

Use this scenario to guide a discussion about sharing your heart. Be very careful not to sound judgmental or accusatory. Remember, your teen is exploring thoughts and first impressions—these aren't actual choices . . . yet. Parents, if your kid chooses option D, don't overreact; he or she may just be testing to see how you'll respond. But don't throw in the towel, either; you're the parent and must set the guidelines that help keep your immature teens from making mistakes they'll come to regret.

Discussion Points

- Why did you make the choice you did?
- What does it mean to say "I love you" to someone?
- Once you say it, you can't get that back.
- While sex is giving away a piece of your heart and body physically, saying "I love you" is like a mental and emotional surrender to another person.
- What more do you have to give to the next person?
- Do you have a different view on this scenario than you did at the start? Why or why not?
- Would you like to change your answer or stick with it?

Love is patient, love is kind. It does not envy, it does not boast, it is not proud. It does not dishonor others, it is not self-seeking, it is not easily angered, it keeps no record of wrongs. **Love does not delight in evil** but rejoices with the truth. It **always protects**, always **trusts**, always **hopes**, always **perseveres**. (1 Cor. 13:4–7)

Parents, tell your teen this story.

You've fallen for your very best friend. The problem is, this person isn't a Christian. With your friend's promises to attend church with you every week and to continue having a heart open to truth, and with your own commitment to being a godly example in the relationship, you think it must be okay—even good—to enter into a committed relationship with this unbeliever. Every rule has an exception, right? Is this one of those exceptions?

Now offer the following options with no personal commentary.

Let your teen think about the choices and make an honest decision.

A. Yes. You believe you can lead this person to Jesus and be a great Christian role model.

B. Someday. You're not going to risk it, but you don't have to throw it all away now, either. You decide to keep praying and waiting. If it's God's will, it will happen the right way.

C. No. It's time to move on. Even hanging out a lot with someone you're attracted to is dangerous, so you'll have to pull back on the intensity of the friendship right now before it leads to something more.

D. It really doesn't matter. You're solid in your faith, so you can date this person without worrying about a shared faith in God.

Crucial Step

Use this scenario to guide a discussion about being unequally yoked. Be very careful not to sound judgmental or accusatory. Remember, your teen is exploring thoughts and first impressions—these aren't actual choices . . . yet. Parents, do you already have a household rule that prohibits your teens from dating non-Christians? If you do not, you'll need to establish one after this discussion!

Discussion Points

- Why did you make the choice you did?
- Read chapter 6 about missionary dating.
- Under what circumstances, if any, is it okay to date an unbeliever?
- Does God have a say in this choice?
- Is there a household rule about dating non-Christians?
- What could happen if an unequally yoked relationship progresses?
- What about dating a believer who isn't as committed to his or her faith? What problems could that cause?
- Do you have a different view on this scenario than you did at the start? Why or why not?
- Would you like to change your answer or stick with it?

Do not be yoked together with unbelievers. For what do righteousness and wickedness have in common? Or **what fellowship can light have with darkness**? What harmony is there between Christ and Belial? Or what does a believer have in common with an unbeliever? (2 Cor. 6:14–15)

PART FOUR

Parent-Teen STUDY GUIDE

Congratulations on making it this far through *Hot Buttons Dating Edition*! This book has dealt with some tough issues and walked you through the practice of using Strategic Scenarios to prepare your family. Now we're going to press in a little deeper and do some work on the spiritual side of choices, sin, confession, and forgiveness.

No matter what the ages of your children are, you'll find some common ground and will learn something about each other through these studies. Visit www.hotbuttonsite.com to find a free downloadable and printable version of the study segment of this book you can use for your personal study. Print off as many as you need.

Choices about dating—the whys, whens, wheres, hows, and whats—are all just that, choices. Parents can do their best to set boundaries and gain the respect of their teens, but ultimately the choice of whether or not to follow the rules is up to the teenager. No matter how perfect a parent is, there is always a way around the rule if a teen wants to find it.

As in anything regarding decisions, sin, and commitment, the action isn't the main priority; the heart is. We can talk our kids to death and somehow convince them to follow our guidance, but if we don't lead their hearts to the cross, their good choices mean nothing in the end. I often use the example of angry people who march and wave signs at abortion clinics. They may prevent an abortion or two by scaring already terrified pregnant girls away from the center, but, without Jesus, that girl is still guilty of murder because her heart hasn't changed.

This book is focused on dating and all aspects of trust and decision making that goes along with that issue. So consider anything that needs to be confessed in regard to dating, but don't stop there.

Confession

Very **truly I tell you**, the one who **believes** has eternal life. (John 6:47)

. . . **Jesus is the Messiah**, the Son of God, and that **by believing** you may have life in his name. (John 20:31)

Jesus said to her, "I am the resurrection and the life. The one **who believes in me will live**, even though they die; and whoever lives by believing in me will never die. Do you believe this?" (John 11:25–26)

If you **confess with your mouth Jesus as Lord**, and **believe in your heart** that God raised Him from the dead, **you will be saved**; for with the heart a person believes, resulting in righteousness, and with the mouth he confesses, resulting in salvation. (Rom. 10:9–10 NASB)

◀According to these verses, what is required for salvation?

Stop and think. Have you confessed with your mouth and believed in your heart that Jesus is Lord? Share the answer with your study partner(s).

◀What does that mean to you to have made that choice?

If you haven't done that but would like to now, take a walk through the following Scriptures. If you're a Christian already, it's still a good exercise to look at these foundational truths as a refresher.

◀Read Romans 3:23. Who has sinned?

◀Read Romans 6:23a. What is the price of sin?

Sin requires a penalty. The only payment for it is death, blood. Worse than a physical death, though, is the spiritual death that separates us from God for eternity.

◀Read Romans 6:23b. What is God's gift?

◀Read Romans 5:8. How much does God love you?

Jesus gave His own life on the cross to pay the penalty for all of our sin. He, an innocent man, took your death sentence and stood in your place, giving you new life in exchange for His death.

◀Read Romans 10:13 and Revelation 3:20. Who qualifies for salvation?

If you'd like to welcome Jesus into your life and receive the free gift of eternal life that He offers, simply pray this prayer:

Dear Jesus, I believe in You. I believe that You are the Son of God and my Savior and Lord. I ask You to forgive my sins and make me clean. Please help me do the right thing, but I thank You for the forgiveness You offer me when I mess up. I give my life to You. Amen.

If you took that step, *congratulations*!

Everything pales in comparison to the choice to walk with Jesus through your life. Now we can apply that choice of confession to the issues in this book and to your relationships.

> Therefore **confess your sins** to each other and pray for each other so that you may be healed. The **prayer of a righteous person is powerful** and effective. (James 5:16)

Confessing your sins *to others* is not a requirement of salvation. James 5 doesn't suggest that you should confess your sins to each other so that you might be saved. Confession to God is the only path to salvation. James 5 is referring instead to healing of the mind, the mending of broken trust, and the repairing of damaged relationships that only comes about by seeking forgiveness from those you have wronged in the past.

Confession clears the air and allows forgiveness to blossom where bitterness once festered. And confession carries healing power no matter what the response is. In other words, your confession starts the healing process in you, regardless of how it's received or if forgiveness is immediately granted.

◀ Work together to write a description of the purpose of confession in family relationships.

Though forgiveness in Christ is complete, sin continues to thrive in the darkness of secrecy. Confession to a loved one deflates sin's power like the air rushing out of a balloon. The sin shrivels, its grip releases, and its power dies. What was once a tool of the enemy to destroy you and your family is now a bonding agent that unites and builds strength and character. What a victory!

When is it important to confess to each other?

- When the issue is causing division
- When there is bitterness
- When you're unable to find peace
- When you need forgiveness

Now is the time to take a risk. You've confessed to God, and you're forgiven of your sins because of the death and resurrection of God's Son, Jesus. Now it's time to lay your heart bare before your loved ones. Trust that we'll get to the forgiveness part of this study just as soon as you turn the page. Let go of the fear of admitting your faults. Confess today so you can be forgiven and see your relationships restored once and for all.

Open your heart and mind, and let the Holy Spirit reveal the things that you need to let out. Let this be a safe moment in your family in which you feel free to lay your heart bare and free your spirit of any guilt or condemnation that binds you.

- Take this time to confess whatever the Lord is bringing to your mind. You may verbalize your confession, or write it in your own notebook or in your study guide (which you can find at www.hotbuttonsite.com).

Trust that your loved ones' response to your confession will be one of forgiveness—the next chapter will lead you through that.

Parent's Prayer

Father, I confess the times I've failed as a parent and ask You to forgive me and help me have more self-control and wisdom when I respond to things. Please help me to be a godly example and a role model for my kids. Give us the kind of relationship that mirrors the one You have with us. Thank You for Your example of unconditional love, continual acceptance, and constant approachability. Make me that kind of parent, and help my family to forgive me for the times I haven't been. Amen.

Teen's Prayer

Dear God, please forgive me for not respecting my parents all the time. Help me to honor the values we've decided upon as a family and uphold them in all things. Give me the strength to say no to the pressure I'm placed under to do all sorts of wrong things. Please help me to be a better son/daughter and make us a loving and united family that serves You together. Amen.

13 **Forgiveness**

Following belief and confession is forgiveness. Ah, what a blessed state to live in . . . forgiven. The very word elicits a sense of peace and calm. It inspires me to take a deep breath and rest for a moment in gratitude.

How about you? Do you feel forgiven?

> If we **confess our sins**, he is faithful and just and will **forgive us** our sins and **purify us** from all unrighteousness. (1 John 1:9)

Do you believe that you're forgiven? Sometimes it hits like a tsunami as the waves of peace wash over the heart. For others, it's more of a steady rain that takes time to feel. It's okay, either way. Whether you feel forgiven or not, you can have faith that you are, in fact, purified and holy before God.

So God has forgiven you, but now what does He expect you to do about other people who have wronged you?

For if you **forgive other people** when they sin against you, your **heavenly Father will also forgive you**. But if you do not forgive others their sins, your Father will not forgive your sins. (Matt. 6:14–15)

◀ What does that verse teach about forgiveness?

◀ How do you feel about that?

Forgiving others is often a simple act of obedience and a step of faith. If you're angry or wronged in some way, you're rarely going to feel like forgiving those who hurt you. Forgiveness, in that case, is a gift from God planted in your heart so that you might extend it toward those who sinned against you.

Would you be surprised if I told you that offering forgiveness benefits you far more than it benefits the person you're attempting to forgive? Surrendering in that way allows God to work more deeply in your life.

◀ Read Ephesians 4:25 and Luke 15. How do you think God wants us to receive someone's confession?

◀ Now, think about this question: Can you truly accept someone's confession and offer forgiveness without holding on to any bitterness or contempt?

◀ What makes that easy or difficult for you?

◀ Read Matthew 18:21–35. Who do the characters in this parable represent? What is the debt? What is the parable trying to show us?

> **Bear with each other** and forgive one another if any of you has a grievance against someone. **Forgive as the Lord forgave you**. And over all these virtues put on love, which binds them **all together in perfect unity**. (Col. 3:13–14)

Parents, name some times you've been forgiven of things in your life and share them here. Try for at least five examples. Spend as much time thinking about this as necessary.

When you see it written out like that, does it give you a different perspective on your teen's sins?

But I'm not God!

What about when it's just too bad, and I'm truly unable to let go of the anger toward someone?

> And when you stand praying, if you hold anything against anyone, **forgive him**, so that your Father in heaven may forgive you your sins. (Mark 11:25)

> Do not judge, and you will not be judged. Do not condemn, and you will not be condemned. **Forgive**, and you will be forgiven. (Luke 6:37)

Believe me, I get it. It's not easy to forgive those who have committed a painful wrong against you and are truly guilty. The problem is that unforgiveness drives a wedge into our daily walk with God. That free and open walk with a loving Savior becomes strained and even avoided when your spirit knows it's harboring something God cannot abide. He talked to His children about this specific issue because He doesn't want it to divide you from Him.

◀ Are you able to forgive each other for the things confessed before God in the last chapter? Are you able to treat those confessions with the same manner of grace that God has shown you? Is anything standing in your way? Take turns sharing.

We've made huge progress through confessing to God and each other, receiving God's grace, and forgiving others. I'd like to encourage you to backtrack a little and dig a little deeper.

◀ What are you still holding on to that needs to be confessed to your family? What sin still makes you cringe when you consider sharing it? Why can't you let it go?

Now's the time to take a chance. Forgiveness is a step away. Families, assure each other that it's safe to unload anything at this time. God has forgiven your sins, past, present, and future—now allow your family to do the same.

Confession followed by forgiveness is a life-changing gift of healing.

Parent's Prayer

Heavenly Father, I'm so grateful for Your grace and forgiveness. I'm so grateful that it extends to cover the mistakes I make as a Christian and as a parent. Please help me forgive others like You have forgiven me so that I can be an extension of Your arm of mercy to those around me. Let me show grace to my children so they will trust me with their sins and their feelings. Help me not to expect them to be perfect, but rather to see them as You see them and readily offer forgiveness at all times. Amen.

Teen's Prayer

Lord, I've done some dumb things—thank You for forgiving me for them. Your gift of salvation has changed my life, and I'm not the same person I was before You came into it. Thank You, too, for helping me and my family work through some of these things. It all makes sense when we talk about it and look at what the Bible says. Help me not to hold grudges against people who have hurt me, and help me to be obedient to You and to my parents. Please help me make good decisions and not to give in to peer pressure. Amen.

For as **high as the heavens** are above the earth,
so great is his love for those who fear him;
as far as the east is from the west,
so far has he **removed our transgressions** from us.

(Ps. 103:11–12)

◀ In light of Psalm 103:11–12, what does the following quote mean to you?

> "I can forgive, but I cannot forget," is only another way of saying, "I will not forgive." Forgiveness ought to be like a cancelled note, torn in two, and burned up so it can never be shown against one.   —Henry Ward Beecher

Confession + Forgiveness = Perfection   . . . *right?*

Unfortunately, I think we all know it doesn't quite work that way. The question I receive at this point in the discussion goes something like this:

"So, if I continue to mess up and the people I've forgiven continue to mess up, how can we live with a clean slate?"

◀ Read Romans 7:14–20. What does Paul do? What is he unable to do? Why is he unable to do it?

Paul is a believer. He's forgiven. He's a mighty servant of God, yet he sins. He wants to do what is right, but he often cannot. He doesn't want to do wrong, but often cannot stop himself.

◀ Continue on by reading Romans 7:21–25.

No matter how committed you are to a clean slate, your enemy, the devil, wants nothing more than to sabotage forgiveness, trust, and peace. He is the antithesis of the love you feel for each other and will stop at nothing to erode it.

There are three steps to combat the devil's attacks.

◀ Read James 4:6–8.

Step One: _____ the devil.

What does that mean to you?

What are some ways to do that as it relates to the subject of this book?

◀ Read Luke 6:27 and Acts 7:54–60.

Step Two: _____ your enemies. _____ for those who have mistreated you.

What does that mean to you?

What are some ways to do that as it relates to the issues you've been addressing with the Strategic Scenarios?

◀Reread James 4:6–8.

Step Three: _____ _____ to God and He will _____ _____ to you.

What does that mean to you?

What are some ways to do that as it relates to the hot-button issues you've been addressing?

Immerse yourself in Scripture and prayer to counter the devil's attacks.

Romans 7 (that we looked at above) ends with a description of the battle between Paul's sin nature and his commitment to God. Good ol' Paul admits that he messes up all the time. But we know that, even though he claimed to be at war with the flesh and struggling with sin, he found favor with God. Let's take a look at Romans 8:1–4 to see the resolution:

> Therefore, **there is now no condemnation** for those who are in Christ Jesus, because through Christ Jesus the law of the Spirit who gives life has **set you free from the law of sin** and death. For what the law was powerless to do because it was weakened by the flesh, God did by **sending his own Son in the likeness of sinful flesh** to be a sin offering. And so he condemned sin in the flesh, in order that the righteous requirement of the law might be fully met in us, who do not live according to the flesh but according to the Spirit.

We have a clean slate before God. It's His promise to us in response to the work of His Son, Jesus. With the slate wiped clean for us, we are able to do the same for others. We're all a work in progress; not a single one of us is perfected and complete. We're complete in Jesus—because of Him—but not because of anything we've done. So allow others the same grace of being "in progress" that your heavenly Father is showing you by keeping your slate free from judgment.

> Being confident of this, that he who **began a good work in you** will carry it on to completion **until the day of Christ Jesus**. (Phil. 1:6)

◀ We looked at Philippians 1:6 back in chapter 3, but let's break it down again. Describe what the phrases in the verse mean to you.

Being confident of this

That He who began

A good work in you

Will carry it on to completion

Until the day of Christ Jesus

◀ How can you apply those truths to yourself and your clean slate before God?

◀ How about others and their slate before you? Is it clean in your eyes? Can you forgive an imperfect person?

From that verse, we're reminded that no one is perfect—we're all a work in progress. Commit to forgiving the failures of others, since you know that you will fail and others will forgive you.

The best way to preempt disappointment is to communicate needs and expectations. Each of you, take a moment to share three needs you have regarding the hot-button issues you've been addressing. For example: "More understanding and space when I'm in a bad mood." I recommend you put this list in writing so there's no confusion later.

Parent Commitments

Speak these commitments out loud to your teen(s):

- I commit to do my best to be a godly example.

- I commit to having an open mind and heart, ready to listen whenever you need to talk.

- I commit to being humble enough to admit when I'm wrong, but strong enough to enforce the boundaries I believe are necessary.

- I commit to _____.
  [fill in the blank based on the needs communicated above]

- I commit to _____.
  [fill in the blank based on the needs communicated above]

- I commit to _____.
  [fill in the blank based on the needs communicated above]

Sign: _____

Date: _____

Remember that your enemy, the devil, seeks to sabotage forgiveness, trust, and peace. It's so easy to stumble down a slippery slope.

The pattern of confession, forgiveness, and a clean slate is perfectly portrayed in the relationship you have with your heavenly Father. He loves you, and wants you to walk in complete forgiveness, confident in His love for you. He also wants you to experience that love in your family.

People fail—they've failed you before, and they'll fail you again. You can't wait for God to perfect those you love, but you can allow His perfect love to cover a multitude of sins—grace from Him to you, and through you to them.

> May God himself, **the God of peace**, sanctify you through and through. May your whole spirit, soul and body **be kept blameless** at the coming of our Lord Jesus Christ. The one who calls you is faithful and **he will do it**. (1 Thess. 5:23–24)

My Prayer for You

Heavenly Father, I lift this family up to You and thank You for their precious hearts that desire to grow closer together. Please guide them as they join hands and walk together in a united purpose to serve You throughout their lives. Facing these Hot Buttons involves release and trust. Help Mom and Dad to use wisdom in knowing when and how to begin the process of that kind of release, and help the teens to respect the boundaries set by the parents and by Your Word. Give them wisdom and strength when it comes to the choices they must make in life. Grant them Your holy sight to see down the road when the way is unclear to them. Help them also to trust each other with some of the tough decisions. As the years go by, remind them of the things they talked about in this book and the commitments they've made to each other. Give them joy as they embark on life with a clean slate. Amen.

Parent's Prayer

Father, I thank You for my family—they're perfect in Your eyes. Help me to take joy in them each and every day—just like You do. You've given us the gift of a clean slate in Your eyes . . . help us to walk in that freedom with each other too. Help me love my family like You do—unconditionally and unselfishly. Please give me wisdom and patience as I help my teens wade through these years. Amen.

Teen's Prayer

Dear Jesus, thank You for forgiveness and for a clean slate. Thank You for a family who wants to serve You and will work hard to make sure I'm on the right path. Please give me wisdom in all things, especially the choices I have to make about these hot-button issues. Help me to do the right thing and to have the strength to stand up to the pressures of life. Amen.

Recommended
Resources

Books

Harris, Joshua. *I Kissed Dating Goodbye*. Colorado Springs: Multnomah, 2003.

Isham, Lindsay. *No Sex in the City*. Grand Rapids: Kregel, 2009.

Jones Gunn, Robin, and Tricia Goyer. *Praying for Your Future Husband: Preparing Your Heart for His*. Colorado Springs: Multnomah, 2011.

O'Dell, Nicole. *Hot Buttons Sexuality Edition*. Grand Rapids: Kregel, 2012.

Risk, William P. *Dating and Waiting: Looking for Love in All the Right Places*. Grand Rapids: Kregel, 2000.

Websites

www.chooseNOWradio.com. The home of *Parent Talk* and *Teen Talk*, where Nicole O'Dell talks with guests about issues teens and their parents need to know about. Topics like peer pressure, dating, body image, self-esteem, friendship, entertainment, and anything else that comes up are covered in a fun, casual environment.

www.choose-NOW.com. The Internet home of Nicole O'Dell and Choose NOW Ministries, dedicated to battling peer pressure by tackling the tough issues and bridging the gap in parent-teen communication.

www.datingadvice4christiansingles.com. A website that gives good advice to Christian singles and couples on dating and relationships in a fun and practical way. Be sure to measure all advice against God's Word.

www.focusonthefamily.com. A global Christian ministry dedicated to helping families thrive. They provide help and resources for couples to build healthy marriages that reflect God's design, and for parents to raise their children according to morals and values grounded in biblical principles.

www.hotbuttonsite.com. The Internet home of the Hot Buttons column, where Nicole O'Dell regularly brings you new Hot Buttons scenarios free of charge, for you to use to foster healthy, proactive communication in your family.

Notes

1. Ray Guarendi, *Discipline That Lasts a Lifetime: The Best Gift You Can Give Your Kids* (Cincinnati, OH: Servant Books, 2003), 301.
2. Robin Gunn Jones and Tricia Goyer, *Praying for Your Future Husband* (Colorado Springs: Multnomah, 2011), 192.
3. Timothy A. Roberts and Jonathan Klein, "Intimate Partner Abuse and High-Risk Behavior in Adolescents," *Pediatrics & Adolescent Medicine* 157, no. 43 (2003): 375–80.
4. Paige Hall Smith, Jacquelyn W. White, and Lindsay J. Holland, "A Longitudinal Perspective on Dating Violence Among Adolescent and College-Age Women," *American Journal of Public Health* 93, no. 7 (2003): 1104–09.
5. From Centers for Disease Control and Prevention, *2009 Youth Risk Behavior Survey*, cited at "Teen Dating Violence," CDC website, http://www.cdc.gov/ViolencePrevention/intimatepartnerviolence/teen_dating_violence.html (last updated February 7, 2012; accessed February 16, 2012).

About the
Author

Youth culture expert **Nicole O'Dell** resides in Paxton, Illinois, with her husband and six children—the youngest of whom are toddler triplets. She's the founder of Choose NOW Ministries, dedicated to battling peer pressure and guiding teens through tough issues while helping parents encourage good decisions, and the host of *Choose NOW Radio: Parent Talk* and *Teen Talk*, where "It's all about choices!"

A full-time author of both fiction and nonfiction, Nicole's desire is to bridge the gap between parents and teens. Her popular Scenarios for Girls series, the natural segue into the Hot Buttons series, asks teen readers to make tough choices for the main characters and offers alternate endings based on the readers' choices.

For more information on Nicole's books or to schedule her for a speaking event or interview, visit www.nicoleodell.com. Follow @Hot_Buttons on Twitter, and like www.facebook.com/HotButtons. Podcasts of *Choose NOW Radio* are available at www.chooseNOWradio.com.